GREY
OWL

GREY OWL

THE MYSTERY *of* ARCHIE BELANEY

ARMAND GARNET RUFFO

COTEAU BOOKS

Edited by Geoffrey Ursell.

Cover photo, COMSTOCK /by Karsh, "Grey Owl – Archie Belaney." Photos on pages 5, 43, 59, 71, 77, 80, 88, 90, 95, 110, 147, 162, 166, and 198 courtesy of Archives of Ontario: collection c273.
Photos on pages 1, 26, and 28, courtesy of National Archives of Canada.
Photos on pages 35, 62, 119, 137, and 208, courtesy of Glenbow Archives.
Photo on page 18 courtesy of National Museum of Canada.
Photo on page 176 courtesy of Donald Smith, University of Calgary.
Photo on pages 33 and 38 courtesy of the author.

Permission to quote directly from *Wilderness Man* in "Lovat Dickson, 1935" has been granted by the Estate of Lovat Dickson. All rights reserved.

Cover design, book design and typesetting by Dik Campbell.
Printed and bound in Canada.

The publisher gratefully acknowledges the financial assistance of the Saskatchewan Arts Board, the Canada Council, Department of Canadian Heritage, Multiculturalism, and the City of Regina Arts Commission.

CANADIAN CATALOGUING IN PUBLICATION DATA

Ruffo, Armand,Garnet, 1955 –

Grey Owl: the mystery of Archie Belaney

Based on the author's thesis.
Poems.

ISBN 1-55050-109-7
1. Grey Owl, 1888-1938 - Poetry. I. Title.
PS8585.U514G74 1997   C811'.54   C97-920032-6
PR9199.3.R76G74 1997

Coteau Books
401 - 2206 Dewdney Ave.
Regina, SK Canada
S4R 1H3

For Judith, who gave me the time,
and in memory of my mother, Barbara Espaniel-Ruffo.

GREY OWL:

THE MYSTERY OF ARCHIE BELANEY

The Trail, then, is not merely a connecting link
between widely distant points, it becomes an idea,
a symbol of self-sacrifice and deathless
determination, an ideal to be lived up to,
a creed from which none may falter.

GREY OWL
Men of the Last Frontier

...an Indian is an idea which a given man has of himself. And it is a moral idea, for it accounts for the way in which he reacts to other men and to the world in general. And that idea, in order to be realized completely, has to be expressed.

N. SCOTT MOMADAY
"The Man Made of Words"

Archival memory.
Paper brittle as autumn, unearthed
across the desk, files scattered.
Words floating like smoke
smell of moccasins you are wearing
warming the bright neon,
carrying you on
to the beginning.

It is past midnight, everyone
is gone, except uniformed security
and you — What is it you are digging for
exactly?
       Note: Archie writes that a beaver's diet
       consists of poplar and birch leaves,
       shredded bark, lily roots and slim branches cut
       into macaroni-like chunks; they also have a taste
       for potatoes, apples and rice.

Transformation and Journey.
Archibald Stansfeld Belaney,
and Grey Owl, Wa-Sha-Quon-Asin.

The people. The names.
George his absent father; Kitty his bullied mother;
Ada and Carrie his spinster aunts; wives and lovers,
Angele Egwuna, Ivy Holmes, Marie Girard, Gertrude Bernard,
Yvonne Perrier; children, Agnes, Johnny, Dawn;
friends and acquaintances, George McCormick, Bill Guppy,
John Egwuna, Bill Draper, Jack Leve, Lovat Dickson,
Betty Somervell, Ken Conibear; adopted family, Alex and
Annie Espaniel, Jimmy and Jane.

The geography.
England. Hastings, a seaside village, his place of birth
at 32 St. James's Road; the move to 52 St. Helen's road,
near the woods he played in; to 36 St. Mary's Terrace,
where he watched the ships move out to sea; Highbury Villa
and his menagerie of pets.

Canada. Toronto, where he worked in Eaton's department store;
Temagami, Bear Island, where he began trapping and married
Angele; Biscotasing, meeting the Espaniels and becoming
a Riverman; Doucet, Gertrude and his first two beaver;
Cabano, where he began to write; Ajawaan, where he completely
became Grey Owl.

Writing to Gertrude, Archie tells her to find out if Alex
is up there. Alex will give her some, quote,
very wise counsel. Heed him, Archie advises.

The mention of family spills inward
that last portrait together in front of the station.
(Taken with Archie's Kodak, your Grandmother said.)
As you turn to the light-blackened window to see
your face transparent as a lens,
and with the click of pen
you find yourself stepping from a train,
through a white hiss of steam,
a snowbound lake vast as ocean,
North,
and there is no retreat.

BEGINNING

Influences

You must speak straight so that your words may go as sunlight
into our hearts. When God made the world he gave one part
to the whiteman and another part to the Apache.
Why did they come together? I am no longer Chief
of all the Apaches. I am no longer rich; I am but a poor man.
The world was not always this way. I have no father or mother;
I am alone in the world. No one cares for Cochise,
that is why I do not care to live
and wish the rocks to fall on me and cover me up.

Cochise, 1866

After school, rather than go directly home to his Grandmother
Belaney's at 36 St. Mary's Terrace, Archie, 11 years old and alone,
walks for miles along the grassy cliff overlooking Hastings
and the English Channel. Come sunset, he heads
for a favourite bluff where he sits with his arms around his knees
and looks west, out past the waves and rising fog,
and dreams of America, of a long-lost father
who in Archie's mind is living somewhere out there
among the Red Indians. The books Archie carries, *Great Chiefs
of the Wild West* and *Two Little Savages: The Adventures
of Two Boys Who Lived as Indians and What They Learned,*
tell him what he already knows, that he too can do it,
and that his real life will begin when he joins his father
and like him is also adopted by the Apache.

With Cochise's words memorized and piercing his heart,
Archie plans his escape, whittles the days into wood.
Lost in a white starched world he cannot understand,
rejected and abandoned, he too wonders,
why things are the way they are,
and wishes deeply with all his will and green strength
for the sea to carry him away. Yes, Apache,
Archie will become an Apache!

Let his classmates jeer as loud as they want, because up here
on this cliff he can see how small they really are, and
he no longer cares what they say about him or his father.
His mind made up, this he reconfirms
as he repeats the words of his hero Cochise,
his thin legs hurrying him back to his Grandmother's before
his Aunts miss him and decide to punish
him with a strapping or, worse,
lock him indoors.

ARCHIE BELANEY, 1899

From St. Mary's Terrace you can see the ocean,
dream the real world, America, like the books say,
out there far beyond Hastings beach
where the candy-striped cabins
are rolled out on their wooden wheels,
and a procession of people take turns changing
into their blooming bathing suits,
bathers tiptoeing at the water's edge.
It makes me want to laugh.

Laugh out loud at the crowd gathered along the boardwalk
staring at the brave few who manage to make it in.
You should see them, parasols and all.
The ladies look like they're going to church
where everyone will be sure to see them,
long dresses and fancy feathered hats,
and the men, they're wearing ties and dark jackets,
imagine, in this heat.

And when it rains, with the wind lashing the trees,
thunder and lightning waking the sky,
then they make sure to lock themselves indoors
like little mice snug in their nests.
While I take to the window and down the drainpipe,
and over to a neighbours' house where I settle in the yard
and hoot and howl ever so faintly
but loud enough to make them stir in their beds.

Why don't I go down to the beach?
Because I'd rather go to Saint Helen's Woods.
There I can make camp beside the creek
and practice with my knife or my rifle,
track whatever animals I spot.
I can pretend that I'm savage and free
and not trapped amongst strangers too afraid to get wet.
Why don't I go to the beach? Because when I finally do,
it will be to board one of those ships
and never return.

STORIES

The Belaney ladies want to know everything.

In their sheltered and proper lives, their Archibald
becomes the centre of gravity. The moment he walks in,
the room falls together in a setting of cups and saucers
as they hurry him to the table to loosen his tongue
with tea and sweets.

Archie goes along (he really has no choice)
and tries to remember all that happened
during the day, much to the delight
of his busy spinster aunts.

And when there is nothing to tell,
to keep them happy, he begins to make up stories,
a whole life of friendship and adventure,
finally stopping only for breath.

An Imagined Country

See this portrait of Archibald Stansfeld Belaney, age 12,
posing stiffly in his dark woolen Sunday suit,
beside his Aunt's collie.

(Never does he suspect
that one day
you will catch him
like this.)

A boy and a dog. Seems pleasant enough. But take a moment
to look into the boy's eyes and ask yourself what you detect.
For this is the same boy who has the ability to see himself
(as you see him) clear across the ocean, all the way,
into the heart of an imagined country called Canada.

SQUAW MAN, 1900

It's the name the boys at school
give him.
He tells them he has Indian blood,
and they say he's cracked.
Call him a Squaw Man.

At first he challenges them
to follow him through St. Helen's Woods;
when this fails, he retreats
into his own wilderness
and locks himself away
on the top floor of Highbury Villa,
his menagerie of snakes,
                    frogs,
                        mice,
                            rabbits
becoming his sanctuary, his refuge
from the collar of Edwardian England,
the cackle of spinster aunts.

His father, his mother,
his grandmother (who dies on him)
and finally his classmates, including
his best friend, Hopkin, who prefers
the pursuit of girls to animals,
all abandon him.

And so, with no one, he creates himself
companionship and dreams for hours
of the life he will lead
among his brethren in America.
Though, never, not once,
despite an ache for someone as big as a country,
does he ever imagine
four or five wives.

AUNT ADA, 1903

Not like that, Archibald! How many times must
I tell you? Now do it again, this time properly.

Each morning Ada makes Archie practice the piano.
Ada breeds collie dogs and believes in strict obedience.
She believes in the old adage: Spare the rod, Spoil the child.
So while Archie plays "Moonlight Sonata" for the tenth time,
Aunt Ada stands over him with a cane ready to crack his knuckles.
Archie will become a gentlemen, even if it kills him.
She will make him everything his despicable father was not.
Their mother had bowed to George's charm and good looks.
She had financed his trips to Africa and America and for what?
Only to have the apple of her eye fester and rot.
Archie too has the Belaney looks.
But Ada will see to it that his upbringing is different.
What is required is discipline. Unrelenting discipline.

If there's one thing I will not tolerate, it's disobedience.
Are you listening Archibald? One, two, three.... Now begin again.

ARCHIE BELANEY, NOTEBOOK, UNDATED

I never went to university, I was grounded
by an ever-blessed aunt. I built on that
by sheer study, but only after many years
of speaking little but Indian.

Buffalo Bill's Wild West Show Comes to Hastings

Indians of the type familiarised by the illustrations
which grace the covers of the penny 'blood and thunder'
publications, Mexican cowboys, handy-men, and cavalry
of many nations, herded together in orderly confusion,
if such a term is permissible, and the demonstrations
they gave of feats of horsemanship, sharp-shooting,
lassoing, and other accomplishments born of long practice
in far parts of the world were indeed a revelation.

— Hastings Observer, August 22, 1903

Archie made sure he was first in line.
He had arranged to go with his friend McCormick.
But all day he could hardly keep himself still.
Five hours to show time he was itching to go.
Finally he couldn't stand it any longer.
He would go on ahead and hold seats.
When McCormick arrived he spotted Archie
talking to one of the Red Indians.

To see them chatting, one would have thought they were mates,
or better yet, brothers. Blood brothers! You know
like in the westerns.

Archie Belaney, 1906

My father, he could be anybody from a bum to a businessman.
On board the ss CANADA I thought for sure I would find him
as soon as I landed. I didn't realize America was so big.
In Toronto I find a job in Eaton's department store, where
hundreds of men come to buy suits and ties and cuff links and
all that stuffiness I had hoped to leave behind. They must
think it odd to see me — this still wet-behind-the-ears
eighteen-year-old — watching them ever so keenly as though
I had never seen a face before. And here I am thinking
he could be anyone of them.

For George Furmage Belaney, 1857 to ?

Father, Father,
who went so far
please speak to me
wherever you are.
You abandoned your first wife
left your second to die
failed in business
after business
and drank yourself dry.

And what of my mother
who had to make do
my brother
and sisters whom I never knew?
Aunt Carrie & Ada
raised me
from age four
but their best intentions
made me run for the door.

Father, Father
It's not easy to forget.
How do you do it
do you ever regret?
When they ask I will say
you're in Buffalo Bill's show.
I can say what I want
they can't possibly know.
Yes, I'm in America
just like you
looking for the one face
I needed but never knew.

North, 1906

In the north
a man's past
is his own

Archie
relishes
the thought

It allows
possibilities
never expected

> In the north
> a man's past
> is his imagination
>
> Archie relishes
> the possibility
> to be

> > In the north
> > Archie relishes
> > the welcome

BILL GUPPY, 1906

My first impression: A decent young fellow, with such
a friendly air and so earnest about becoming a guide.

Last stop Lake Temiskaming. I'm waiting at the station
to pick up a load of supplies when he walks right up
and asks me for a job. He's determined, says he'll do anything
as long as it'll take him into the woods, a real foreigner
calls the bush the woods. Why ask me?
Somebody's pointed him in my direction. As a guide
and trapper I got a certain reputation in these here parts;
some folks call me King of the Bushmen.

Long and lean, over six feet, he's wearing work clothes,
corduroy pants, a heavy shirt with a red hanky
around his neck, an old felt hat tilted sideways.
I like his look, his readiness, and so we strike a bargain
and I take him on. He'll stay the winter and work for his grub
and come spring we'll paddle to Lake Temagami. Should see him
light-up when I tell him Temagami has 600 miles of shoreline
and a good 1,200 islands and mention it's home to the Ojibway
of Bear Island. Eyes just like a Hudson Bay fur-buyer
who knows he's getting what he wants — for next to nothing.

He's keen and pumps me for information.
He has to know everything. Me, I'm surprised
what he already knows — he's got no fear of wild animals
and certainly no fear of being alone in the bush.
We come to call him Professor, because he's so well-mannered
and articulate. Did I mention after supper he plays our piano?
A regular wizard at the keys, rattling out tune after tune.
Somebody has obviously raised him well, though he won't
talk about his home for the life of him.

TRIBUTE

She marks him as one would initial a tree.
And he learns to bear the scar. To love
books and music, find friends in birds and rabbits,
squirrels and snakes. From her he learns
how to present himself, charm with manners and bearing,
impress with knowledge, affect with simplicity and finesse.

And so he dedicates his first book to her.
Even uses Beethoven's "Moonlight Sonata," her favorite,
as one of the musical selections in his lectures.

He never denies his Aunt Ada. Her influence
can be likened to a log wafting through black water,
imperceptible but solidly there. She helps him
to make something of himself, and he is grateful.
Who he denies is Archibald Belaney.

ARCHIE BELANEY, 1907

The dark waves bellow over the deck of the ship and soak
me through. It took such an effort to get away from Hastings.
Why am I returning? The thought loops across my mind like
a caged bird flopping from bar to bar. Money's a problem.
Most of what I earned in Toronto was stolen.
I can't imagine my grandmother or aunts giving me more.
I hate the thought of even asking. But what else can I do?
I still haven't found work in the woods, no one will hire me.
One look at me and they call me sonny and make fun of me.
The old-timers can tell I don't have any experience — it's
my accent — the moment I open my mouth to ask for a chance,
they roll their eyes like this ship. One way or another
I'll get rid of it, if it's the last thing I do. So why
am I returning?

Admit it. You're going the wrong way. What you've got to do
is tell somebody. Tell them you've made a terrible mistake.
But the evening's dark and cold and there's no one on deck.
Then look up towards the bridge. Shout to the captain
to turn the ship around. No. Wait. Hold it. You can't.
They'll think you're stark raving mad. Calm yourself.
Instead, clench your collar and look back out to the sea.

But I can't, because all I see out there is Highbury Villa,
my childhood home: the heavy furniture in the drawing-room,
the stiff high-backed chairs, the piano by the French doors
which open to the garden, lilies and roses in blue Venetian
vases, tea-time with silver and china, white linen napkins
on a tray.

Then close your eyes and think of the cold spray you felt
on your canoe trip from Temiskaming to Temagami, before you
a wealth of pine-shadowed hills, afternoon light slicing
through stands of silver birch, reflecting off water
brilliant as diamond. Yes, these are the riches I want.
Is this not in fact freedom?

Another week tossed in these gale strong winds and home. Surely I could have survived on my own, found work. What unanswerable, invisible force draws me back? Nature calls the birds thousands of miles through such weather. And just as they have no choice neither do I. This voyage is meant to be — call it one last visit. Even so, I wonder how long I can endure it?

On Archie Belaney's Return to Hastings, 1907

MARGARET M^CCORMICK, CHILDHOOD FRIEND

He looks more Indian than ever, and leaner,
clad in an old loose suit and a wide brimmed hat.
He insists on wearing moccasins at all times, and
swings along the street with a loping gait — hardly
the same person.

GEORGE M^CCORMICK, CHILDHOOD FRIEND

He never calls to say goodbye. Three months later
I hear from his Aunt Ada he's returned to Canada,
and after him bringing me a pair of real Indian moccasins.
Mysterious chap.

HENRY HOPKIN, CHILDHOOD FRIEND AND CLASSMATE

By chance I meet him out walking along the sea. I ask him
what he's been doing, but for some reason he's reluctant
to answer. Finally he tells me he's working as a guide
in the north country, which to me seems odd since he only left
for Canada last year. I ask him to visit, but he never does.

Archie Belaney, Notebook, 1907

The sidewalks hurt my feet. My mother has remarried and
is busy with her new baby. My aunts are the same chatterboxes
as ever. The town and everybody in it is the same as ever.
I feel shackled by so many old emotions
I swear
      I will never return.

GITCHI-SAGANASH (TALL WHITEMAN)

The Tema-Augama Anishnabai become the source.
Finally he has found a people, the deep water
people, to slake his unquenchable thirst. As
often as possible he paddles to Bear Island
to learn their language, their lore, the stories
he will later use to remake himself.

As for them, they welcome him and his interest,
give him the name Ko-hom-see, Little Owl,
the one who takes in everything. They smile
when they see him moving over the dark water,
his white face as bright as a blaze on a tree.

To Become

She belongs to the caribou clan
and moves with grace
                    and vigilance.
She watches
him struggling with himself
and takes him in her strong arms
and says she understands and will help
make him
one with them. He wishes
but finds it difficult to believe
and laughs that it is he
who will make her.

While she sleeps, he lies awake,
fixed to an iridescent night, alive
with her breathing
                    moon and stars.
When he turns to her he notices a pale light
cast upon her face
and over her flannel nightgown.
This frightens him. How long
will it take before she begins
to act like him?

How long? He wonders and sits up
as though already hearing the onslaught of hammers
shattering the lakeside calm.
Only yesterday he got a job
                    to help build a new lodge.
Another lodge means more tourists
which means more money,
for guides and cooks and waiters and janitors.
Jobs for her,
her family,
for all the Indians,
as servants in their own land.

In Memory of Angele, Belle of Temagami, 1908

How does he meet her? Is it at the Temagami Inn
while he's working as a chore-boy and she as kitchen help.
Dawn's hooped light flares his red imagination,
and so he teases her, throws potato peels.
All for a shy smile.

Or is it during his run as mail carrier? A winter
afternoon near Bear Island, a dog comes snarling
at him, and he reaches down with an open hand
and turns it into a pet. Then she appears,
like an apparition, wrapped in a snowy shawl.

Maybe it's at a summer dance. His eyes trail her
all evening. When it comes time, he bids on her basket,
goes higher than he can afford, but he doesn't care
because it means he will share her supper, outdoors
where the moon is their only chaperone.

What we do know is that he met her before
she had ever been with a man, when she stood tall
and slender, looked much like her daughter, his
daughter, before long years of heartbreak
and poverty. This we know.

Archie Belaney, Notebook, undated

Goodbye: the thing is
to keep looking ahead.
The moment you look back
you're done for.

ARCHIE BELANEY, 1912-14

You haven't been to Biscotasing? Boy, are you in for a surprise.
Folks there — in Bisco that is — are the friendliest folks
you'll ever meet, people who really know how to kick up their heels
and live. Indians and whites alike, I mean everybody
talks about Bisco (Hey! It's got a population of 200 or so.)
like it's the centre of the universe
and for a Riverman maybe it is, on the headwaters
of the Mississauga, Spanish, Mattagami and Groundhog Rivers,
some of the wildest water known to man. Like they say,
it's the place to go — if you're tough enough
to join the canoe brigades and can handle the action.

And so one morning I tell my wife Angele I'll be gone
for the summer — I'm off to find work — and from Temagami
I start paddling some 75 miles due west.
By this time not only have I learned how to handle a canoe
(which doesn't mean I still don't have a lot to learn), but
by now I can curse, drink, dance, make love, throw knives,
and generally raise hell with the best of them.
And that's exactly what I do — when out of the bush
I whoop it up with the Boys, you know the regulars
(and become pretty popular if I do say so myself),
when in it, I stick close to the old timers, the Rivermen,
and pick their brains, learn as much as I can from them.

Life is freedom in Bisco. So free I decide to stay and
not go back to Temagami. During the winter I take to trapping
and send a few dollars back to my wife.
It's the least I can do. I mean I want to go back but...
another winter comes and goes, and I'm back on the river
and then... things happen which I've no control over.
War breaks out in Europe.
I get piss drunk and in trouble with the law.
My girlfriend gets pregnant.

What to do? What else but get going, escape. The law,
the women, the past, get rid of it all.
Escape and join the Army. (Besides it's my patriotic duty.)
It's the way out. The way to lose myself,
while setting myself loose,
like a canoe roaring down a funnel of water.
Someone who knows how to shoot,
whose mother was an Apache,
whose father was a Texas Ranger, can be useful in the Army.
At least that's what I tell them.

George McCormick, Montreal, 1913

Around Christmas he calls on me at the Royal Bank.
His rooming house turns out to be a flophouse
near the station. The old green window blind
keeps rolling itself up until he gets furious
and yanks it off the frame. Wretched, he says
with a little laugh. We've had a few drinks
by then so I don't think much of it.

He asks about his Aunts and the old Belaney gang,
but as I'm telling him about Hopkin getting on
as a reporter, he decides he doesn't want to hear
any more. Abrupt and rude, he suddenly dashes
my words aside and rushes on about canoeing
on some river he calls the mighty Mississauga.
Finally exhausted, breathless, he draws heavily
on the liquor.

Undoubtedly, by this time he has gone Indian,
shoulder-length hair, a large felt hat, buckskin
jacket, moccasins. His voice too has changed,
now having assumed a Canadian accent. And to think
that merely eight years ago we were fast friends.
Under that strange exterior, there walks a torn man,
I say to myself as I shake hands for the last time
with a perfect stranger.

BILL DRAPER, 1914

Profession: Adventurer, Sailor, Forest Ranger

We spend the summer paddling the Goulais River
patrolling the forest reserve.
How does he explain away his hint of English accent?
Easily.
As a kid, Buffalo's Bill's show took him to Britain,
where he met his father's two sisters,
living la-de-da fashionable in the outskirts of London.
Congenial old birds, seem to me, because they put him up
and give him an education.
And educated he is, recites original poetry
and always carrying a pad of paper to take notes,
a good listener too.

MARIE GIRARD, 1913-14

Everybody tells me not to go. But I don't listen.
I'm working as a maid at Mrs. Legace's hotel.
Archie comes by and plays the piano.
Nobody can play like Archie, music you can float on.
That winter I quit my job and go into the bush with him.
What can I say? He's handsome and sensitive.
I'm young and in love.

Come spring when we return to Bisco, and he goes away
to work as a Fire Ranger, he's still in my heart.
When I hear he's been drinking and causing trouble,
I say to myself, Oh, that Archie. I don't think
it's serious. I don't know he's pulled a knife.
I don't know the police are after him.

It's dark when he comes knocking at my door.
He has to hide and asks me to come with him.
He says it will be just like the winter before.
We'll live together: it's my dream.
Again I go, and he keeps his promise.
We have it wonderful together.

September 26, 1915, our baby is born, a boy
like Archie — who by this time is long gone.
The war, he never said, I didn't know he would join.
Still I'm happy. Sounds silly but I have my memories.
My only wish — knowing I have TB — to see Archie
once more before I die. What can I say?
He was different. Me, I was young and in love.

Authority, Authority, Everywhere, 1915

I

They make me a lance-corporal
because of my previous experience
in the Mexican Scouts, 28th Dragoons,
and store my silver six-shooters for safe keeping.
Then they put me in the Royal Highlanders of Canada
and order me to wear a kilt. Indians don't wear skirts,
I cry out, and beg to ask them, How
they can expect us to win the war without pants.

II

The minute I return from visiting my aunts
they rip the strip from my arm and yell, Belaney!
Go absent-without-leave again and you're one dead Indian.
I can live with that.

ARCHIE BELANEY, 1915-16

You want to talk civilization. OK
let's talk War. On August 6th, I join the 13th Battalion
and because I can handle a rifle I'm sent promptly
to the trenches.

One black night I hang my greatcoat
on a branch sticking up in the mud,
in the morning a dead man's green arm
hands it back to me.

I see a man trying to stuff his intestines back inside himself.
He asks me for help.

Chlorine Gas: Blisters your lungs.
                  You vomit blood.
                  No mask. Piss in a rag
                  and stick it in your face.
                  No piss. Borrow some.

They make me a sniper. I get to see the tears
the second the bullet rips through them.

The shelling, it makes my brother Hugh go mad.
Now his life is a room where he sits and pounds
his exploding head.

I'm lucky. On April 23rd, I'm wounded in the foot
and sent away to have a toe removed. Later I'm discharged.
Some accuse me of shooting myself. Others say impossible.

After

by now death and fear is gangrene
rain, mud, cold, inside out everywhere
the end of the world with no end
in sight   makes you pray like Christ himself,
with your soul, with each word,
that if you are spared
as sure as God can strike you down,
you'll repent, change, become
whatever they want
you to be
then one day you're on your way home,
your promise in hand, you marry
much to everyone's pleasant surprise,
even your own
but it doesn't last   for you,
there is no peace.

ARCHIE AND IVY

Married February 10, 1917 —
Separated September 19, 1917

A child wants candy.
Archie wants Ivy,
a professional dancer,
internationally travelled,
interesting and attractive,
twenty-six and single.

Should he or shouldn't he?
He already has a wife
and child,
already has a girlfriend
he's left
pregnant.

Before him sits lovely Ivy,
slender legs crossed,
auburn hair held back
with delicate long fingers,
as she tells him about Hungary
asks about Canada.

Should he marry her?
He could return
alone
establish himself
in northern Ontario
and then send for her.
A good plan.

He has known Ivy since childhood.
A London girl born
and bred, someone
with whom he can spend an afternoon
at the zoo
but a lifetime in the bush:
who is he fooling?

Ivy Holmes Belaney, 1917

When I visit him he has all the glamour a wounded soldier
can possibly have for a young dancer, lines of pain drawn
into his dark handsome face. One visit leads to another,
and before long we fall violently in love and decide to marry
as soon as we can. His foot is damaged and the doctors order
him to stay off it. I invite him to put his weight on me.
And he does and we enjoy each other as though February 10,
our wedding day, is the end of time.

It's not, tomorrow comes, and I begin to find him strange,
secretive, almost reclusive. He begins to hobble around
on crutches. Begins to go down to the seaside to watch
the waves. Insists on going alone. When his discharge
comes through, he leaves for Canada. He says he will write
but never does. What went wrong? I keep asking myself,
we never argued or fought once.

Archie Belaney, Notebook, undated

Twelve years old. I was Big Chief Thunderbinder
and she was my Dancing Moonbeam. What happened?
How to explain? Start with recognition of
human selfishness.

ESCAPE

When he was dry
he drank,
dandelion wine,
white alcohol,
vanilla extract,
his own stink homebrew,
even shoe polish once.

Back in Bisco Archie's demons ran wild,
so fast he couldn't keep away from them,
from his shack to the tracks and back, limping
painfully on his wrecked foot, pleading, crying, even
singing for them to stop, and when they didn't he stumbled,
cursed and fought.

He did all he could to drown them, all but overturn his canoe
— it was his saving grace — Ojibway taught, he got a job
as a Forest Ranger and escaped on the Mississauga River,
swift and deep.

BILL DRAPER, 1920

Stories about Archie, I've got a sack full,
each one more wild than the last. Do you know
about the time he was drunk in church?
Blasphemy. You say. What he saw happening
to the land was blasphemy.

You got to understand. Fur prices had skyrocketed;
the new railroad was bringing in pseudo bushmen
by the train load, greedy hunters,
                prospectors,
                trappers of the get-rich variety,
                were like an invading army;
lumber companies, such as big J.R. Booth of Ottawa,
were busy licking their chops, swallowing vast stands
of white pine, spitting out a no-man's-land of chewed waste;
mining companies were just as rabid, ripping and gouging
with their machinery and dynamite.
The war in Europe was over. The war here had just begun.

ARCHIE BELANEY, NOTEBOOK, 1920

Moccasins on,
for the first time
I could feel the earth under my feet.
Home from the war with my right foot shattered
I can't wear anything else.
Henceforth, I will always feel the earth.

ALEX ESPANIEL, 1920

Everybody can see plain as day he's suffering.
Maybe a better way is to say there's something chewing
at his insides, the beast of war hunched and hissing,
all that he's seen and done over there in the trenches
coiled inward.

We do like the rest and just watch him.
      (nobody wants to get too close
      especially when he's drinking)
We see him fall to all fours, snarl for more
drink, scream when he doesn't get it,
watch the icy fangs dig in.
Devilish, my wife says. Call it Weendigo.

Then one day we see him sprawled outside his shack
shivering, too weak even to get up and feed himself,
and my wife says, Look at the pitiful thing won't you?
He's got to get back into the bush, I say,
and my son puts him over his shoulder
and we take him to our camp
on Indian Lake.

JANE ESPANIEL, 1923

He's sitting on a stump back of the house.
I'm standing behind him. There's a pail of the NO-TOX dye
mixed with water on the ground between us. I put a piece
of old canvas around his neck so I won't make it black.
His hair's long, down past his shoulders. He's just washed it
and between my fingers it feels fine, not like Indian hair.
I hold some of the wet strands in one hand and with the other
proceed to wipe them with a rag that's been soaking in the dye.
The process takes about an hour. He says make sure to do a good
job around the scalp; the roots are always the first to show.
I tell him if he doesn't keep still I'll scalp him and
he won't have anything to worry about.

He laughs, then becomes pensive, as if cast far from the shadows
of the surrounding bush we call our backyard.

A Trapper's Trade Is To Kill

What they teach me is how
to make a clean kill,
how to drown them as quickly as possible.
The winter hunt is the best,
kill the mother in the spring
and the little ones starve and
you destroy your source of replenishment.

What you want to do is guide them
towards the bait with a couple of poles
plunged into a hole in the ice,
they go for the bait and
snap they hit the trap
and cannot make it back to their house for air.

Sometimes when they come to the surface
they can be clubbed,
not a pleasant task
but easy enough to do,
a judicious bullet is also an effective method
for getting the job done (though it costs a bullet).
Either way it's your preference.

JIM ESPANIEL, 1922-25

I guess you can say he's part of the family. Not only
does he spend the winter on the trapline with Dad,
and the summer working as a Forest Ranger with me,
but he even moves into our house and lives with us
for nearly three years.

It takes us 21 days to tour the area by canoe. Though
one time we go from Birch Lake to Bisco in one day,
that's 75 miles with our canoe weighed down
by hundreds of pounds of gear.

Archie always takes along his notepads.
We work from 4:30 in the morning until 9:00 at night
and as soon as we're finished, he starts making notes.
Where we've gone, people we've met, animals, weather.
It doesn't matter how many miles we've paddled, he's never
too tired to jot something down. When we're back home,
he uses these notes. He writes fast, fills a large pad
in no time and then rolls it up and files it away.
He has nearly a packsack of material by the time
he finally leaves Bisco.

ARCHIE BELANEY, NOTEBOOK, 1923

The camp was without women except a few of those ladies
who like their whiskey straight and their cards crooked,
thus providing an illuminating example to the Indian
of the benefits to be obtained from civilization.

ANNIE ESPANIEL, 1923

He comes in all serious,
sits down at the table beside me and
says he's organizing an Indian War Dance
for Queen Victoria Day.
Me, I smile to myself when he tells me this
and look at the long face he makes.
So I say Archie, What's an Indian War Dance? None
of us Indian people have had one of those recently.
For Archie that's OK.
He's going to take care of everything.
He'll show everybody
what they're supposed to do.

Of course he needs my help to make a special suit.
You can't have an Indian War Dance without a costume.
I agree, and he brings home some brown material
and red ribbons from the lumber company store.
He draws me a pattern and I make it up for him.
When I'm finished he paints on little arrows,
adds animal teeth and bones.
He does a good job.
It's when he makes a drum out of a cheese box
that I have to shake my head.

ARCHIE'S WAR DANCE

He'd have a couple of drinks
under his belt
to make him dance
better
at least he thought
he danced better.

War Dance Given At Biscotasing
by Jack Leve, fur-buyer
— *Sudbury Star, May 30, 1923*

The Chief began his death song by beating his drum,
singing and mocking the prisoner; then Chief and council
held a conversation in their own language and decided
his fate. Finally the Chief spoke in English and told
the prisoner of the wrongs that the whiteman had done
to the Indian. After this was over, he lit a fire and
the entire tribe began their torture dance by beating
their spears, knives and tomahawks by the flames. Then
they danced around the prisoner, letting out wild yells
and stabbing him with their weapons. The dance and torture
lasted for about fifteen minutes after which time the Chief
addressed the prisoner and told him that he admired him
for being a brave man and therefore would let him go free.

Great credit is due to Mr. A. Belaney for acting as Chief
and organizing the performance.

JACK LEVE, 1923

Archie's incredible. His speech hushes everyone,
going on about how badly Indian people have been treated,
the decimation of the animals, the destruction of the land.

He amazes me. I never imagined he could speak like that.
I don't think he did.

ANNIE ESPANIEL, 1925

When he carries on, hooting and hollering
around the Bisco station, the Anglican Indians
call him Nottaway, which means Snake.
Nonsense.
The old people say, If you lose something
and you go back and look carefully,
you will find it.
Archie just hadn't learned how to look.
I'm a religious woman myself.

"Unlawful conduct in a disorderly manner whilst drunk
at Biscotasing Railway Station."

—Warrant for Archie Belaney,
issued by the Justice of the Peace
at Chapleau, Ontario, 1925

ALEX ESPANIEL, BISCOTASING, 1925

He paddles to our place by moonlight,
skulks in and says he's got to go. The police
from Chapleau are coming to arrest him.
I tell him not to worry.
His singing and drumming isn't that bad.
And if he's been staggering around again
and making a nuisance of himself,
throwing knives
at passing boxcars,
they'll just give him a fine.

He says it's time to go anyway.
So I give him some dried moosemeat,
a couple cans of beans,
flour and salt for bannock,
and a few dollars.
He isn't sure where he's going
or when he'll be back.

Then one day I get a letter
from someone named Grey Owl,
and when I open it up it's Archie.

TRANSFORMATION

Gertrude Bernard, Lake Temagami, 1925

Together we are pilgrims of the wild,
at least that's how he portrays us.
And for the most part it's true.
Are not lovers pilgrims? feeling
their way through each other.

You be my Jesse James. I'll be your Pony.

You have to be at least twenty-one to work at Camp Wabikon,
but I get a job because my father has entrusted his little Pony
— my childhood nickname — to a guardian, the social manager.
Come fall, I'm off to a convent school in Toronto,
and although a rich doctor has offered to pay my tuition
(He likes my looks.), I need the money from waitressing
for living expenses. They say an education will open doors,
and I can't wait to go.

One June morning Archie shows up in his canoe looking for a job
as a guide. At first I don't like him, a real know-it-all.
And he lets on that he doesn't like me, calls me (spoilt) kid.
But we soon strike up a truce, and as soon as we do
my niece dies, and I have to leave Wabikon and return home
to Mattawa.

(Now that I think about it, I couldn't have escaped him
if I had tried.) His presence flies with me; lying in bed
with the curtains pulled aside, I think of him every night.
Who is this handsome stranger, this wilderness man
with long flowing hair and tilted fedora, fringed buckskin
and red sash? He's the man of my dreams.

He certainly makes an effort to get to know me; he's not shy,
far from it. But who could imagine him already having two wives
the way he plucks up his courage and strides up to my father's
door? He shows me a silver revolver and says he's hiding out
from the law, says he's been charged with attempted murder.
Back in Bisco he took a knife to a man who raped a young girl.
Before that he punched out a station-agent who swindled him
out of a job.

He tells me this, and I see a modern Jesse James
sitting in our little living-room, and I can't help but love
every noble inch of him. He's leaving
to go trapping up north and hops a freight train on the outskirts
of town — to avoid the crowd, he says, as only a desperado can.
A week later I began to receive his letters, thirty-page
stories filled with Nature's beauty and his heartache. Again
he asks me to come to Doucet for a visit. Then one morning
I wake knowing I must go, and I pack my knapsack and tell
my father that I'm no longer a kid.

And so I join my Jesse James and give myself over to his
imagination, become his heroine, his Anahareo.

SIMPLE ADDITION

A is for Archibald
A is for Anishnabeg*

A + A = Archibald Anishnabeg

B is for Belaney
B is for Beaver

B + B = Belaney Beaver

now simply add A + B

A + B = Archibald Belaney
       Anishnabeg Beaver
       Archibald Beaver
       Anishnabeg Belaney

* the Ojibway people

BILL CARTIER, 1925

Well what yea know, the same old bunch from Bisco.

We're up near Doucet, Quebec, me, Jim Pichette, Ted Cusson,
Archie Belaney, where we hear there's lots of marten and
lynx. Ontario's closed now to everybody except Indians
who come from the area. Even Belaney can't trap there,
him being a half-breed Apache. So together we all move on.

Come fall Archie asks us to help him build a cabin away
from ours, down a little trail. He doesn't come right out
and say he's building it for her. But we know. He's not
even sure if she's going to come but wants to be ready.
Looking at him, we know he's happy. Me and the boys tease
him, but not too much because he's got a temper. What could
she see in a wild son-of-a-bitch like him, we wonder? I mean
he's already 36 and she's only 19. Anyways we finish the cabin,
and he christens it Pony Hall, after her.

One moonlight February evening, low and behold, she appears
fresh as a snowflake, young and beautiful. We're surprised,
no, shocked's the word, wondering what she must be like. Archie,
he's grinning from head to snowshoe, like he knows all along.
Mr. Confident, that's what we call him, that's how he appears.

This is my wife Gertie, an Iroquois Chief's daughter,
21 years old. Tall, slim & very strong.
A woman of great courage & a true partner.
Well-educated, talks perfect English; everybody likes her.

— *Archie Belaney in a letter to Aunt Ada, 1926*

How Do You Know?

Because she's the one who tells her father
she'll be gone for the day
joins you
and never returns.

Because she knows how to let the past go,
and encourages you to do the same,
to open yourself as you would your cabin door
to the medicine winds of spring.

Because she has wings, transparent bright wings,
that you want so much to hold and tame
you sit up nights watching her sleep
your arms aching with emptiness.

Because she lets you call her beautiful Insect
even though she carries her share
and doesn't complain
she's not used to snowshoeing 70 miles.

Because she cooks so deadly you're afraid to eat.
Drinks and plays cards.
Argues fiercely
and goes for your revolver
to shoot up your moosejuice party.
Stabs you
with your own skinning knife,
then cries hysterically seeing you hurt.

Because this is the woman who somersaults your life
who can't bear to watch you club beaver to death.
Who makes you see, as she sees,
the suffering you inflict.

How do you know
she's the woman?   Because:
she's the only one who beats you to the draw,
and walks out on you.

GERTRUDE BERNARD, 1926

The campfire blazes and glows like a Weendigo's huge eye
and around it we sit consumed by sight, as though this
is where we belong, as though we have journeyed
all our lives to be here, or have always been here.
In silence the story spreads and becomes
as much a part of us as the crackling logs
and glowing embers, the wings in the trees,
the footsteps behind our small circle of light
and warmth, spreads and becomes our heart,
blood, eyes, thoughts, becomes us.
And we nod as each word sinks and tears
like a hook in our mouths
as we taste, swallow, digest, and swallow again,
trying not to get sick
or mad as hell.

In Cree Country.

The Lac Simon people explain in their broken English
that two trappers from town poisoned the bush,
used strychnine for bait and didn't bother to collect it
come spring. So happens their huskies ate it and died.
These people depend on their dogs
and can't afford to buy new ones. With the onslaught
of white trappers clearing the area of everything
that so much as moves, beaver, marten, lynx, fox, wolf,
you name it, they can barely make ends meet.
What little they earn goes to pay their debt
at the Hudson Bay Company store.

No fur, no money, and now no dogs.

How did we come to be here? Where does dream stop?
I remember we had gone into Doucet to the train station
to cash in my ticket. I had decided to stay.
We were going to get married, or as Archie says spliced,
when this short thickset Indian comes up to us,
introduces himself and says Archie's the man he wants.

His people need Archie's help.
We'd never set eyes on him before
and yet we went along. He seemed to know
we would. How? Later when I asked Archie
he said that once when he was fighting fire
one of the old timers took out his drum.
He sang. He drummed. That's all he did
while the rest of the crew worked to beat hell with shovels
and axes. And you know what: it started to rain.

How?

It was the younger men, Nuna says, as he pokes the fire
and makes sparks fly. Sometimes they don't think.
Of the consequences, I add, looking away from the burst of heat
realizing I've interrupted. Cultivate the art
of listening (Listen, damn it!), Archie always says.
Frustrated and angry
with the way their trapping grounds are being destroyed,
they sought revenge for their dead animals and burnt down
the shack of these whitemen, poured coal-oil over their traps,
which sent them scurrying into town and to the police.
The two Indians responsible are now in jail
facing a possible two-year prison term.
You will speak for them when they go before the court,
Nuna speaks with finality, offering Archie a smoke.

You who can, must.

There are so many beginnings. Stops and starts. Shifts
of direction that after a while it seems we hardly know where
we're going. We think we're settled, comfortable at home with
our families, our work, our plans, our lives, but sure enough
something happens: someone just happens to beach his canoe
near where you're sitting (as Archie happened to do),
or just happens to sit beside you on a train,
or happens to walk up to you to ask the time of day,
or says it's you I need, and

then everything changes, everything, and before you know it
you're off. Again? Yes. Travelling
full out into wind, rain, sleet, or sun,
neck craned forward, arms and face wide open
as though attempting to embrace and swallow time itself,
ready to soar, going, going, gone. But where to?

How can you possibly know?

Of course Archie takes on the task and speaks
like he's never spoken before, or maybe he has,
for in a way his words remind me of the letters
he has written me, I mean the power in them.
We're all piled into the one-room town hall
and after the charges have been presented and the judge asks
if the defendants have anything to say in response
to what has been brought forth by the plaintiffs
— who are looking sorrowfully wounded, I might add —
Archie jumps to his feet and calls out that yes he does
have something to say, and if his Honour would permit him
to speak he will explain exactly why
it is these furry-faced culprits who should be charged
(he's pointing at them while he says this) and not
the two young Cree who are indeed victims
of an unconscionable callousness driven
by nothing less than insatiable greed and scorn
for our weaker brethren, the defenseless wild beasts,
and more, the Indian people who depend on Nature
for their very survival. For certainly
the use of strychnine is illegal. Well
you can imagine the judge's face
hearing this halfbreed trapper dressed in braids
and buckskin speak like Moses himself.

In well-enunciated English.

Instead of two years the Indians get a month. And
after a feast of moose meat, bannock and tea in our honour

we're soon on our way heading 60 miles due west.
If there's one thing Archie won't tolerate
it's talking while paddling, and still I try to speak
to him about his accomplishment. He refuses to say much,
only that it was something he had to do
and while doing it realized the utter futility of it all,
like trying to patch a rotten canoe
instead of just building a new one. But you're wrong, I exclaim.
You did good. They would have got a lot stiffer sentence.
I can't see him in the stern but sense
that he's giving me his same old grin,
as though I am completely and foolishly naive,
merely his little Pony, his little Insect, who, blinded
by the campfire, forgets the bush is all around, doesn't see
the stir of the predator, the submission of the weak,
claws clamped tightly around a neck, the meek little squeak
that does no good. Is that it? Cat and mouse,
and he feels that he has merely squeaked
a little louder than usual.

But the drum, I want to turn and tell him.

Instead more silence. The silence that connects, the unspoken,
is more, means more, draws like a lightning rod.
This I learn afterwards as does Archie, when we finally
enter Lac Simon and spot a summer tent town, white canvas
and Hudson Bay blankets like flags in the distance,
smoke, fires tanning and cooking, women talking and sewing,
men fishing or repairing. Around a point
and we are greeted by an old man, with long flowing white hair
and piercing dark eyes, who waves us to shore.
We beach our canoe, and he takes hold of the bow
and steadies it while we climb out. Then upon clasping hands
with Archie and telling us his name, Papati, and
that he is Chief, he says he's been waiting for us.

Waiting for us? But.

How did he know we were coming? There is no explanation,
and we are hard-pressed to find one. And so we try
our best to ignore it and settle in and rest, until
the day before we are to leave, when Papati says
it is time for him to marry us.
And again we are spun around into a new direction,
a new start, a direction which up until now has hovered on
the edge of dream. For me there is no turning back,
no waking up and going home.
Here too we arrive at a point of recognition,
through a lake of fog to a familiar jut of land,
a secret place we have known deep in our mind's eye,
where we are meant to be. All I can say is
we are again brought face to face with all
we don't know or understand, at least I am,
as for Archie, let's just say the experience
of it all (which includes our marriage),
all the coming and going, the words and silence,
confirms his conviction. Not the futility,
but more the possibility,
the power and mystery.

We paddle hard throughout the next day without a sound.

What You See

What you see are the sorry
remnants of those who blunder
the job, set their traps
so the beaver can twist
out, leaving behind shattered
bone and sinew, condemned
to survive with limbs
cut and wrenched off.

What is worse than seeing
these industrious little
people try to prepare
for winter, build
house and dam,
collect food with stumps
instead of hands and feet?

What you mustn't neglect
to mention are those who
dynamite the house or violate
with poison, leaving
senseless destruction.
What is it all for?
a livelihood? a quick
buck? What kind of men
are these? It makes
you wonder.

Gertrude Bernard, Doucet, 1928

Ask me what I see from the cabin window — nothing.
Nothing but endless bush: trees, trees and more trees.
What do I hear? What else but the crash of falling snow,
lengthening another lonely day in and day out.
It gets so I don't even want to drag myself
off the bunkbed. Nothing to look forward to
except Archie coming home, cleaning and oiling his traps,
looking over his damn maps, planning his next trip.
Hate, how else can I describe my feelings
about this monotony? this excuse for a life, and, yes, I admit
I've even come to resent the man who brought me here
to live so-called happily ever after.
I'm young! damn it — young — I remind myself, my frustration
bursting into tears.

Soon we're at each other's throats.
We don't speak except to argue.
I'm leaving, I tell him, and swear up and down and sideways.
If that's what you want. Go, go right now, he says,
swinging open the door, letting snow fly in.
Don't think I can, eh, I say, and rush across the room,
grab my coat and snowshoes.
I'm a couple of miles away before I finally stop for breath
and turn and see him in the distance with that same look
on his face that tells me he wishes there was something he
could do for us.

In the spring the kittens are born   helpless
little balls of fur   barely clinging to life. Archie says
only the worst kind of trapper hunts in the spring. But
he has no choice. Prices
have fallen so drastically, it's either trap or starve.
What else can he do? I tell him we can leave, find work
somewhere, maybe move to town.
He says he'd rather starve.
He's a trapper, whether I like it or not. I don't like it,
not one bit, but there's nothing I can do. His mind's made up.
Again his hands become death.

One day the sun rises dripping warm, and the hunt's over.
Archie sees my need to get out, how happy and excited I am
that the killing season is finally over, and invites me
to come along with him to collect the traps.
When we arrive at the last beaver house, we discover
that the mother has drowned in the mud with the trap.
To my delight the kittens are alive. We catch them,
and I put their furry little bodies inside my shirt.
Archie says they'll fetch a good price.
This time we argue all night and into the morning.
Listen, I'm talking to you, he says, arms crossed, chin rigid.
Not TO me you're not. You're talking AT me again, I scream,
holding back my tears. I repeat: we're not selling them.
Wait and see, he says with extravagant calmness.
And I stare at him so hard he has to turn away, and I go
to the kittens playing on the bed and take them in my arms
like children.

Archie does his best to ignore them.
Now that he's out of the bush and around the cabin all day,
he's afraid of becoming attached.
On the day we are to bring them to town one of them gets lost,
and we search for it all afternoon until Archie finds it
in a muskeg swamp. Neck deep in muck, arms stretched out,
one hand on the squirming beaver, the other on a willow
for balance, he calls for help; and after handing me the critter and
pulling himself out of the suck, to my surprise, rather
than get upset, he begins to laugh. And it's at this moment
I detect not the hardened trapper but instead Archie the boy,
grinning as though he's just found a new pet.

Back at the cabin, he goes to bed while I wash his clothes.
That evening, the same little beaver, after meticulously cleaning and
combing himself, decides to thank Archie by climbing up
onto the bed and sticking its wet little nose into Archie's face.
Moved by the gesture, he says, almost casually, as though
it means little, that he's reminded of the pets he used to keep
as a child. But as he tells me this, it's plain to see
memory has brought back a pain
he keeps well hidden.

And with the simple stroke of his hand, the child in him
reacts and jumps to the animal, and once again,
like all those years ago, he finds himself seeking refuge
in the source of the only sanctuary
he has ever loved and depended upon —
the small and helpless —
and the heart that has been stone hardened
with all these years of wilderness living
suddenly and unexpectedly splits wide open.

We do not sell.
Instead we give them a home, and they become our family
and, in the end, Archie's destiny.
McGinnis and McGinty, we call them.
Two personalities.
Two people.
Beaver people.

ARCHIE BELANEY, 1928

She loves them. I love her. How can I not also love them?

I can't remember when I've seen her this happy.
Now that they're part of our lives she doesn't wait
at the window, staring into the snow, complaining
she has nothing to do. That's to say the least.
The little buggers keep us going from sunrise to sunset,
chewing legs off tables and chairs, scattering flour,
stealing my papers. Regular little cyclones those two.

I know the idea of a beaver colony sounds far fetched.
But maybe it's time I at least try to give something back
after all my years of taking — that's what Gertie says.
Anyway as far as trapping goes, it's over, it's dried blood.
Where I easily made two thousand a season, money enough
to throw a helleva good party, I can now barely pay my grub stake
at the store. Last season I still owed eighty dollars.

I cross a lake in the pitch of the afternoon and silence
snaps through me. It's eerie with not a sign of life.
Beaver dams neglected, houses abandoned, scattered heaps
rotting like buffalo on the prairie. There's nothing alive.
Nothing's moving. No tracks anywhere. The country seems dead,
and maybe it is.

ARCHIE BELANEY, PRESIDENT, TREASURER,
AND SOLE MEMBER OF THE BEAVER PEOPLE SOCIETY, 1928

It's easy to say NO,
NO MORE,
I'VE HAD IT,
THAT'S IT,
THE END,
END OF IT,
to talk big, boast you don't depend on it,
to go ahead and quit
the beaver hunt,
or any kind of hunt.
But what comes next? What happens
when the money runs out?
What about feeding yourself
                    and your family?

Can't make ends meet on a measly army pension.
Over and over, What to do?
What to do? And before long
your thoughts are as heavy as spring snow
you find yourself trudging over on snowshoes.
Maybe
you could simply ask for donations
and they'd come flocking in, tens, hundreds
                    thousands. Maybe
Pony could strike it rich
up in northern Quebec and return
loaded with enough gold to keep you
and the beaver for life.
Maybe you could write Nature articles for those magazines
and actually make enough to live on.

They tell you to move to Temiscouata country,
over New Brunswick way, where (according to reliable sources???)
there are so many mink and lynx and marten and whatever...
they fight over which one wants to get caught first,
and as for beaver, why they're so thick
they've taken to living on land.

Good place for a beaver colony, good place to trap
—if one must — good place for you.

So with all ANDS,
          BUTS,
                    IFS shoved aside
you and Pony book passage to Cabano
and arrive only to be greeted by miles of twisted slash,
the timberland clear-cut and emptied
of any kind of life.
With no choice and eight hundred pounds of supplies,
you end up rushing through fifty miles of this ravaged terrain
to get to Birch Lake, where you hear the bush is still alive,
doing your damnedest to beat November freeze-up
which hits hard:
you wake to half a foot of snow and ice.

Then, with six miles to go,
the river we're following suddenly becomes a shallow creek
and you're forced to travel overland.
Without help, bone weary,
you have no choice but to carry
a portion of your provisions at a time, constantly moving back
and forth as you go, tearing down and setting up
your frozen tent
in the blowing weather,
eating ice-hard bannock — only your dream, the warmth
of your single vision sustaining you.

But sure enough, one evening, you find yourselves breaking
into fits of laughter, hugging one another: You've arrived
and to your utter and dizzy amazement, it's all behind you;
the grueling haul is over.
And for a while you don't care what comes next
(that you still have to build a cabin), you're far too relieved
and happy just to know your Beaver People Society
is a hard-earned step closer
to becoming reality.

BIRCH LAKE, 1929

Strange to see this trapper's cabin
carefully set in grove of tall dark pine
bordered by graceful pale birch. Here
a tame moose comes calling, a tiny doe,
a fat muskrat named Falstaff, not to mention
the regular brigade of whiskey-jacks.

The people inside are never alone.
Two beaver commonly called the Macs
also live there and do much
to keep the party lively. Strange,
in the heat of the winter season,
to see no skins stretched
across these walls.

JEAN NOEL, 1929

It's a large important looking envelope with Country Life
written on it real fancy. The return address tells me
it's from England. We don't get many foreign letters
here in Cabano, so I take special care not to mix it in
with the general mail and put it all by itself on a shelf
below the cash register.

March, *il fait un froid de loup,* it's bitter.
They got a couple beaver living with them out there,
so I know they won't come to town until the weather warms up.
Sure enough, towards the end of the month spring finally
arrives and so do they, pulling their toboggan. As usual
he asks for his army pension cheques, and that's when I show
him the letter. She gets all excited and tells him to go ahead
open it. Him, he takes his time and examines it closely,
before pulling out his big knife and slitting a corner.
And wouldn't you know it, as he opens the letter,
out flutters a pink cheque just like a pretty little bird.

There's also a magazine — which she grabs and tears open.
And before I even know what's going on, she starts jumping
and squealing. Look Archie, look, she says, while he reads
his letter. Then she runs over to me, points to a page
and says, My husband wrote this. I don't know what to say,
first time I ever heard of an Indian who can write.
As for him, he takes my pen and signs his cheque real fancy like,
same as the English letter, and we all have a good laugh.
But me, I'm wondering what kind of Indian is he?

Colonel Wilfrid Bovey, 1929

Forty years old and nearly destitute,
he comes to Metis-Sur-La-Mer hoping to find work
guiding and to publicize his proposed beaver colony,
and ends up staying in a tent on the beach.
Metis is not the kind of resort that employs guides,
and he's reduced to exhibiting his beaver for ten cents
admission so that he can buy a little food. His wife,
who can't be much more than twenty, comes to the hotel
looking for work as a maid and proudly informs us
that her husband has recently published an article
in *Country Life*, the well-known English magazine,
which quite frankly impresses us. So we ask her
to bring some of his work over and later agree
to engage him to speak at the Seaside Hotel.

The material itself is powerful with its passionate
conservation message, but of course we are skeptical
that a half-breed from the bush can speak before an audience.
The turnout is good, over a hundred people,
and he arrives on stage looking quite dashing and,
I might add, even theatrical in his fringed Native attire.
He's clearly nervous and stumbles through his introduction
as he tries to read from his notes. The crowd is impatient
for him to get on with it, just as he appears to be
impatient with himself, constantly turning his attention
from his notes to the audience and back, losing his place.
But before anyone is aware of what is happening, has time
to applaud his daring, he gathers up his papers and
clenching them in his hand moves the lectern aside.

Then, with a calm intensity that makes me recall the sky
just before one of those blankets of storm we have up here
appears out nowhere and sweeps across the lake, with
that kind of captivating force, he begins to tell us a story,
as though we were sitting around a campfire. And all at once
a hush pervades the audience, lightened from time
to time with jolts of laughter — the beaver people
with all their antics are alive and busy; the wild north

has blown into the room carrying the smoke of ancient
ceremony — and he has everyone eating out of his hand,
like the animals he's telling us about, his papers
by this time forgotten on the floor.

They collect seven hundred dollars that night
and have over a thousand by the time they leave
and it's only the beginning.

ARCHIE BELANEY, 1929

Afterwards I tell Pony,
as soon as I got on stage
and saw all those silver-dollar heads beaming up at me,
their expectation cracked open like a full bottle of gin,

I felt I'd swallowed an icicle

(which is putting it delicately
if not mildly,
because suddenly I felt I'd sat on one).

DAVE WHITE STONE, 1929

Archie and me go back all the way to Ontario,
trapped and guided rich Americans with him,
which gets me to thinking I'd rather have a guide,
than be one. So I get it in my head to go prospecting.
Hey! Why not? Can't Indians get rich or is that the reserve
of white people? Sure they can. That's why I show up,
to visit and have a few laughs for old-time sake
before saying goodbye. I'm off to Chibougamou country,
where I'm told one old Indian made himself a gold necklace
out of flattened nuggets. Would just slip off a piece
when he needed to buy something. Took his secret
to the grave.

You should see Gertie when I tell her this. She's squirming
to go with me. I'm old enough to handle myself, she says.
Me, I'm old enough to be her father, and I tell Archie
I'll take care of her. He doesn't say anything,
it's our way, and our silence binds us. In the meantime,
his two little Irishmen, McGinnus and McGinty don't show up,
and we spend the next week searching the bush.
I'm surprised because up until now trapping's been our life.
The search proves hopeless, but Archie won't quit
until I manage to find another kitten, take it in my arms,
like I too might never trap again, and bring it to him.
Funny how things work out. The Indians go searching for gold,
ready to tear up Mother Earth, and Archie stays behind
to take care of the animals. Indian, can't say he is,
can't say he isn't. Speaks the language though.

How

It starts slow,
a little kindness.
The kind that begins
in the shelter of your arm,
a basket made into a bed,
a bit of food. Trust
takes time. It's
a luminous bird
slowly descending from the stars
to the tip of your fingers.

The process of naming
stamps personality,
tells and seals,
and there is no longer dependence
but interdependence.
Some ask to buy,
but there's no way
you can think of cash
for indentured bondage,
zoo slavery.

In their eyes you see
your own capacity,
as fathomless as the wilderness.
But through two tiny animals
how is it possible?
Then one night they don't show
and you search for weeks,
follow trails that deadend.
Until finally, exhausted,
you have to stop
and admit love.

Indian

Country Life wants a book
and you've agreed to give them one,
but the writing doesn't come.

So you force yourself
by solemn oath
to remain seated,
leave only when you must,
to check on the beaver,
chop wood,
fix something to eat.

You even erect a table beside the bunk
so you can reach at all hours,
jot down an idea,
      a word
         an image.
And still nothing.

Inspiration
that's what you need,
so you turn to drink and before you know it
you've got an empty bottle of vanilla extract
hanging from a cord around your neck
like some kind of broken charm.
Your mind a forest fire
blazing out of control.

And nothing fits.

Grey Owl?
Wa-Sha-Quon-Asin?
Archibald Stansfeld Belaney?
Whiteman? Redman?
Who's speaking? You yell
as you now break your pledge and stand and rush
to the mirror and make your Indian face.

Who are you speaking as? Who are you
speaking for? You rip the noose
from your neck and fling it into the corner.

Outside in newborn snow,
without any thought of where you're going
but aware you must go,
you strap on your snowshoes and move
across the lake. Until embraced
by pure night,
you stop to catch your breath,
and become aware.
You've nearly lost sight
of your cabin. Even your tracks.

Around you pines sway in their untouched whiteness;
above, the sky dances the dead;
below, its shadow, the lake swims alive.
This is what it's all about.
Why worry about who you are
when you already know
you are but a moment
of this harmony, little
more than a snowflake of it.

What you must do is simply act, and be.
Return to the cabin, move
towards the light,
the wind calls as it chills you through
and fills your lungs
with voice.

BERNIE GRAHAM, 1929

He's now coming into Cabano almost every week,
either to mail an article or see if there's a cheque,
and as we are one of the few English speaking families,
he brings over fresh venison or fish and stays for supper.

We can see the loneliness tearing at him. His wife Gertie
has left again, this time to go up north prospecting.
He says he doesn't blame her now that he's writing every day.
What can he expect? She's eighteen years younger and wants action
and adventure and refuses to be cooped up in his ordeal.

Still, this recognition does little to relieve his ache.
And so he comes to our house seeking diversion when he can't
stand the silence, when it storms loud and his mind sinks
deep into past winters, and he finds himself yearning for her
and those distant happier times she represents. Times like this
his animal friends can't help him, them with their mute
kind of language.

What he needs is the company of his own kind and so we party
long into the night with Archie playing piano and us
singing at the top of our lungs. Sure we have a few drinks.
Archie likes his drink. Sometimes he makes his own moonshine
out at the cabin and sometimes he comes with us to Riviere-du-Loup
to buy beer. There's also a potent brand of vanilla extract
he particularly likes.

But today there's a hefty cheque from *Canadian Forest and
Outdoors* magazine, which for Archie means OK it's party-time.
He's roaring after being broke for so long and buys a bottle —
Archie likes his gin when he can get it. Later we go for supper
in a fancy restaurant; we're really flying high.

It's when we're about to order that he overhears them.
The French Canadians call him *Sauvage,* a name he detests.
I'll show them, he says, and with his upper lip curled, his eyes
as cold as the blade of his knife, he orders his meat raw
and then proceeds to eat it with his hands. Snarling
at anyone who dares look.

ARCHIE BELANEY, 1930-31

The current is faster than I expect.
Suddenly my articles break into demand.
Letters of congratulations come flying
in from across Britain and the United States
(few from Canada which I find disconcerting).
Strangers want to visit me.
Reporters want to interview me.
They announce that I'm the first
to promote conservation:
the beaver,
the forests, the
Indian
way of life.

I begin by signing my name Grey Owl,
and saying I was adopted by the Ojibway,
and that for 15 years I spoke nothing but Indian;
then, before I know it, I have Apache blood.
Finally I'm calling myself an Indian writer.

Fast, it all happens so fast.
At first I'm hesitant.
I'm unsure of the name, the sound of it.
(Although, do I not prefer traveling at night?
Did I not hoot like an owl in Bisco?)
I think of the risk, those who know me.
There are Belaneys in Brandon.
My wife Angele in Temagami —
who knew me when I still carried an accent —
not to mention all those folks in northern Ontario.

But the thrust of self-promotion is upon me,
and head first into it, I hear myself
convincing myself that nobody's going to listen
to an immigrant ex-trapper from England,
promote an indigenous philosophy for Canada.
And if this is the only way
to get Canadians to listen,
then I'll do it, and more
if I have to. I'll be
what I have to be.
Without hesitation.

What I Didn't Say

Before I know it, they're calling me a saint!
and I crumple the newspaper, clench my fist
and bang
bang the table and hiss
that I'm one of the worst bastards
who ever walked this good Earth.
If those asses only knew the half of it.

But because I'm the first to question
what it means
to cut down life,
to say leave some wilderness for our children,
leave the Indians what is theirs,
they think I should be wearing a white robe
with a halo around my head
like some kind of damn trophy.

They neglect to mention I didn't say ban hunting
(or fishing for that matter).
A beaver kills a tree to live. In nature
life and death fit together like teeth,
or maggots in meat left to rot.
All I'm advocating is respect.
Stop the barren greed,
the parade of slaughter.

GERTRUDE BERNARD, 1930-31

It gets so that I have to tiptoe for fear of squeaking
the floorboards, muzzle myself from any spontaneous outbursts,
and always, always, the constant scratching of his pen.
During the summer I put up with it by amusing myself outside
with the beaver, Jelly Roll and Rawhide, but come November,
that's it — I've had enough, suspended between life and death.
And so I tell Archie that a chic resort has just been opened
in Montebello, and I've decided to go and find a job,
maybe drive a dog team for rich tourists. He says go,
even though I can tell he wants me to stay.
I leave the next day.

Then one January evening I get an urgent telegram from Montreal
telling me to meet him at the Windsor Hotel at once.
I'm instructed to go to the front desk and ask for Grey Owl.
A bell boy in a red suit escorts me up to the room, and sure enough,
it's Archie — decked out with a feather in his hair. He's been
waiting anxiously for me to come and provide what he calls
moral support and upon seeing me holds out his arms for me, for
the room, and says, Well Pony what do you think?
Impressed, more like flabbergasted, it's not a room at all,
but instead a lavish suite, satin curtains and all.
And so I ask him, What's going on? Did you strike it rich?

I'm lecturing, he says without further explanation.
He's pressed for time, and I'll have to see for myself.
I can already see he's had a few drinks to calm himself down.
Ah, you'll do fine, I tell him, holding back any doubt.
Remember your talk at Metis? You were great.
That was small stuff. This is the Canadian Forest Association's
annual convention, big time. They're paying the shot, he says,
and I can also see that despite his apparent uneasiness
he's basking in all the attention they're lavishing on him.

On the podium Archie is a natural. A transformation occurs
and he is no longer merely Archie the reformed trapper
but someone he calls Wa-Sha-Quon-Asin, Grey Owl —
He Who Walks By Night — who speaks and acts
like a great Indian orator of old. The audience is awed
or better yet hypnotised and won't let him sit down,
until he finally tears himself away. Poetry, some call it.
An encyclopedia of natural wisdom, say others.
Before Grey Owl can even think of leaving Montreal
he's wined and dined by high society and from here
it's onward and upward with more invitations to speak,
more requests for articles, more publicity.
The accolades come pouring in, and Archie, I mean Grey Owl,
drinks them up feverishly.

To Be A Red Indian

Red skin.   Black hair.   Piercing eyes.

Feathers.   Beads.   Moccasins.   Braids.

Always slouch.   Never smile.

Say How-Kola

JAMES HARKIN, OTTAWA, 1931

Potential is as good a word as any to sum up what Grey Owl means
to the Parks Branch. At the forestry convention his talk
about the spiritual life of a tree ignites the evening,
and yet he speaks with such reverence and conviction
the audience cannot help but clap enthusiastically.
The Canadian Forestry Association — a tough acorn to crack
if there ever was one.

And so as Commissioner for National Parks, I hire him
(a bit of brilliance on my part)
to be our Naturalist — another good word.
My plan is to station him in a park, provide
for his beaver colony and use him and them for publicity.

He's writing a book. His articles in *Country Life*
and *Canadian Forest and Outdoors* are attracting attention
both here and abroad. The film we've made
featuring his beaver Rawhide has been sent to schools
across the country, and shown as a short in movie houses,
and what's more, it's a hit with young and old alike.

Asset, an even better word.

I'LL TELL YOU HOW IT GOES

You sit down with a raw shiny pencil
in front of a large blank-looking writing pad
and get all settled, and no ideas come, nothing.
The writing pad looks at you expectantly
and says Well, and you say Well, and a most helpless
feeling comes over you.

There is only one thing to do and that's to begin
writing something, however foolish it seems to be.
You start correcting yourself, and before you know it
you get interested in what you're saying.
Then you're all set for six months' work.

ARCHIE BELANEY, NOTEBOOK, UNDATED

Conservation: Must appeal to man's selfishness.
                Start with a recognition of it.

Tolerance: The right of every living creature
                to follow the path laid out for it
                by the Master of Life.

Security: I do not value it.

A white sun, feathery wisps freshen the trail. You
have just passed through a narrow avenue of snow-dressed
pines and naked birches, and now splintered light makes way
to a horizon of sky that begins at your feet. You're awkward
on these damn snowshoes and nearly cross them and tumble sideways
into a drift as you descend onto the lake. He's in front pulling
a loaded toboggan, you are behind doing your best to keep up
to his long effortless strides.

How much further, you want to call out, but don't dare.
Then rounding a point that sticks out like an exclamation mark
from the margins of bush, he stops and points down to what looks
like an ordinary embankment, until he wipes away some of the snow
and shows you the air hole of a beaver house. He bends close
to it and in a soft voice that you would use to talk to a child,
he rouses the inhabitants. Mah—W-e-e-e-e, he calls, and sure
enough after a moment comes a faint cry. Before leaving he cuts
a couple of saplings and thrusts them into a hole in the ice and
turns to you and, says, with the semblance of a grin that almost
cracks his stone-steady gaze, A little snack.

And before you know it, he's off again bounding in front of you.
By now it's dusk and the bush begins to reshape itself in fading
light. Over there, he points, and in the distance you can see
a cabin with a welcome of smoke rising from a tin stove-pipe.
You let out a sigh of relief and breathe easier between pants
of breath. Then, without warning, his hands cupped around his
mouth, he begins to hoot, hoot, the sound, hollow, lifts over
the lake into darkened trees. This you should have expected.

At the door you are greeted by a young woman with a firm handshake,
short black hair, riding breeches and a leather fringed jacket.
Boyish is your first impression. Inside, with kerosene lamplight
flickering off the walls and windows, you cannot help
staring at the dark intensity of her eyes, her curved
softness. It's beauty you now perceive.

The one room itself is crammed, disarray reigns, fishing tackle, traps, boxes, bags all vie for space. Hooked from the walls are clothes; across the two bunks blankets and more clothes; on the table paper and pencils scattered among plates, knives and forks. And amid all this, a most amazing piece of furniture, in the corner a full size beaver house which they've covered with a green tarp to keep the dust down. He tells you the beaver are inside sleeping off the winter and it's then that you notice all the teeth marks on the table and chair legs; even the door has been gnawed.

That evening you feast on bannock, bacon and molasses beans, drink huge cups of steaming tea. And he talks while you listen to his voice amid a blizzard blowing outside. He's squatted over by the glowing stove, his arms clasped around his knees, light casting red over his face and braids, as he tells you about his life as a trapper, of Bisco, and the Mississauga and her men, of blood-sweating portages, and the beaver and what must be done to save them from extinction. It's not until dawn is stretched

in the room that you finally go to sleep, taking Grey Owl's bunk,
he rolled in a blanket on the floor. At noon you awake,
have more bannock and tea and then head out to check
the country and do some ice fishing for supper.

As for Gertie, she comes along for the change. She's bored
and shows it, and tells you she will not stay much longer,
which makes you think, It's too bad she can't be more like him,
as content, as Indian. For you, life here is new and fascinating.
But by the end of the week it's time to return to Ottawa.
Your assignment is over, and you are anxious to tell the world,
your friends in government. Yes, you have met the famous
Grey Owl, a true wilderness man, an Indian in the flesh who fits
every image you have ever had of what an Indian should be,
someone who has beat civilization, who has found peace
and tranquility within himself, who has found
himself. He will receive your highest recommendation.

"the adventurous career of grey owl
(wa-shee-quon-asier)"

In 1905 or 6 or thereabouts he left the band of Jicarilla Apache
to which his mother belonged. His father and grandfather before
him were free trappers and Indian fighters up and down the West
from the Canadas to California. Grey Owl's father served as a
Government scout and guide to waggon trains at various military
headquarters and frontier posts, including at Fort Laramie, when
Colonel Cody (Buffalo Bill) was chief of Scouts at that post.
The injustice and unfairness of the wars against Indians
eventually drove Grey Owl's father to retire from this work,
and he went to England with Buffalo Bill's first show, taking
with him an Apache woman (Grey Owl's mother) as his wife.

On leaving the band, Grey Owl hired with Buffalo Bill and spent
nine months in England with him. Tiring of this, he quit, and
influenced by his father's tales of a trapper's life, Grey Owl
came to Canada, around 1906 or 1907. He took to the bush
in time to participate in the Cobalt Silver Rush. Next he became
a trapper, was formally and ceremonially adopted by the Ojibway
Nation, learned their language and methods of travelling and hunting,
being now more of a bush Indian than he ever was
a plains Indian.

Johnny Jero, 1931

My mother was Marie Girard,
my father, I never met,
Archie Baloney.

When It Comes

There are rumours, bits and pieces,
dry as tinder, ready to catch fire
and burn me at the stake.
          (Confess! Confess!)
So when they hint to ask:
          pardon me, but is it true?
I look them in the eye,
straight as a good paddle,
as though they could trust me
with their life.
And I say: I feel as an Indian, think
          as an Indian, all my ways
          are Indian, my heart is Indian.
What more can be said? What more
is there? When it comes.

How in the world could a half-breed trapper pick up such
an elegant style?

—Prof. W.T. Allison in a review of
Men of the Last Frontier, Winnipeg
Tribune, July 16, 1931

ARCHIE BELANEY, 1931

The review accuses me of having a ghost writer
and, even though I take offence,
I do,
the other side of myself.
The half I don't consider Indian, although
by now I feel that side also slowly darkening.

To explain — why I can write —
I simply announce to the press
although my mother was a Jicarilla Apache,
my father was an American scout named McNeil
with a sister in England, who is to be credited
for providing me with a sound education, and to whom
as a gesture of gratitude, I have dedicated my book.
A half-breed who leans towards his Indian side, I explain,
and they're satisfied just looking at me and my scowl.

As far as I'm concerned, it's not a question of Who,
that's not the issue, but rather How.
How do I get away with it? Again, a simple answer:
you see, it's not me they see at all;
it's the face in their mind,
the one they expect (of me),
born out of themselves,
in their own image.

LOVAT DICKSON, 1932-38

When Grey Owl's first book *The Men of the Last Frontier*
is finally published in 1931, it is an immediate success
on both sides of the Atlantic. Surely an oddity, a book
written by a half-breed, though one might say it sets
the publishing world ablaze. An earnest and vivid portrayal
of the Canadian north-land and those who inhabit it,
the reviewers overwhelmingly conclude (with the exception
of one or two skeptics who refuse to believe).

And so when he writes asking me to take him on, easy to say
I jump at the chance. He says his publishers had the audacity
to change his grammar and syntax, not to mention the very title
of the book, without his expressed permission. Far more
concerned with nature than with man, he had wanted to call
the book "The Vanishing Frontier," the emphasis thus placed
on a vanishing nature. To his mind, their actions only confirm
man's insensitivity and self-centeredness.

He's up in arms so to speak and will no longer have anything
to do with them. He says he wants me and doesn't care if I'm not
established. He's got word I'm a good and honest Canadian
and that's good enough for him. Besides, I'll understand
where he's coming from, he says, and won't try to fit him
into a quote "literary mold." He says he's already neck deep
into his next book, which he'll call Pilgrims of the Wild, and
I too am suddenly deep in ambition. Though I remind myself
one wrong move is all it takes.

GERTRUDE BERNARD, 1932-34

I return from six months of prospecting in northern Quebec
to help Archie move to Beaver Lodge. I don't intend to stay,
in fact I'm planning another move myself, somewhere, anywhere.
What I really want to do is strike it rich (Who doesn't?)
but that's not the only reason I go,
want to go, need to go. Blame it
on the magnetic core, the pulse
that drives a bird, the inside
of an untamed river, blood
red, rich and alive.
Blame it on me.
On him.

You can't stop me, I tell him.
One way or another I'll go, and he knows it,
with or without his backing.
Besides how can I even think of staying
when Archie himself complains of the monotony?
The government cheques roll in, and we come to a halt,
even our food is delivered on schedule.
With the beaver sleeping what else can he do?
Write?
As far as I'm concerned, I'd rather die
than be bound to the swampy stagnation
of another book. I can already hear it,
the static of his scratched voice,
over and over,
       SHUSH,
          QUIET,
             PLEASE, I'm trying to.

But stop me he does. Before I can leave
I discover I'm pregnant,
which to me means trapped,
that I'm one with all the other helpless
creatures he's so determined to protect.
I stay until summer — how do I? — and then Dawn

is born. By now the books and the beaver,
Jelly Roll, Rawhide and their kittens,
have completely consumed him.
He's ripped the roof off the cabin to make a film
and stays up all night
        writing about them
        watching over them.
When I return from the hospital with the baby
there's another cabin built for us
so we'll be more comfortable, or
should I say, out of the way.

Nine months later I'm back prospecting
and before I know it 400 miles away
as the crow flies.
Up to God's Lake, Manitoba, with stops
                in Waskesiu,
                        Lac la Ronge, Fort Stanley,
                        Reindeer Lake, Flin Flon,
                        The Pas, etc. etc. etc.

Dawn's in Prince Albert, Archie's at Beaver Lodge.
I don't see either of them until 18 months later
when I return to find Archie busy memorizing his lines,
wound up like a spring-loaded trap.
He's about to set sail on a speaking tour
of Britain so we barely have time
to say goodbye.

ARCHIE BELANEY, NOTEBOOK, 1932

They have rated me the best outdoor writer there is and
the greatest authority on Canadian wildlife and forest lore
living today. Yet there are better bushmen everywhere;
the people I learned from for instance. And I tell them
that too, giving the Indian about 90% of the credit.

CALL ME

What I want to know is
what makes her think she can take off
for OVER A YEAR,
write two or three times, and then come waltzing
back
as though she's been away for a couple of weeks?

She wants to spend the winter in Prince Albert; fine,
that I can understand;
sure it's boring here.
But she doesn't even hint, say one single word,
she's not coming back
as soon as the ice breaks up.

I give her shit: Who in hell do you think you are?
And call myself sucker.
She doesn't reply
until I write again and ask her to forgive me
and come home.
What I want to know is after all this time
how does she know she can get away with it?
Know how much
I'm alone.

What got into me that night? All I remember
is walking up and down some road howling.
Hope I didn't make too many breaks.

*—Archie Belaney in a letter
to Gertrude Bernard, 1934*

Vamoose

Go. Go. Go. Go. Go. LEAVE ME ALONE.
Once and for all. Once and for all. Once and forever.
Don't think I can live without you? Is that it?
Well I've got news for you. Let me tell you something.
You're in for the shock of your life. Not only
am I going to live without you, I'm going to enjoy it.
Understand what I'm saying TO YOU. Goodbye.
Right now. There's the road, use it. Good riddance.
Don't look at me like that, you damn bitch.
You asked for it.
You wanted it.
You got it. And if you don't understand plain English
then understand this... Beat it. Vamoose.
For mercy's sake.
Leave me in peace.
Let me forget.
Go. Go. Go. Go. Go. I SAID LEAVE.

W-A-I-T !!

Why I Retreat (When Anyone Comes Too Close)

One face is truthful
The other lies.

One face gives
The other takes.

One face is kind
The other cruel.

One face remembers
The other forgets.

One face is gentle
The other rages.

One face cares
The other neglects.

One face is open
The other sealed.

One face heals
The other hurts.

One face is handsome
The other ugly.

One face changes
The other remains.

November 17, 1934

Dear Gertie: My Anahareo

I will think of you Christmas eve Gertie (O excuse me!)
and hope you will find some cheer? Happiness on that Day
we used to celebrate so sincerely, all alone. I guess Dawn
our lovely daughter will be the best off of the family, being
with Mrs. Winters and her family in Prince Albert, which ought
to make us happy and not too lonesome.

There will be Christmas bells in the spruce tops here
with the wind in them, but there will be no one to hear them
but me. All the same, my Christmas will be the best one a person
could have in the knowledge that I have perhaps contributed
a little, ever so little, to the happiness of each and every one
of my real friends — and they are not many; they could go on
the fingers of one hand and are rather widely scattered — and
that I have done my best for those dependent on me.

Oh and Gertie, you must keep up your end and not deny your
identity as Anahareo when the book (Pilgrims of the Wild) comes
out, especially as I have paid you considerable tribute and
made you the heroine — and a little more womanly than you
actually were.

You should see the letters I get from publishers!

Yours Affectionately,

Archi-bald! (not yet)

ARCHIE BELANEY, NOTEBOOK, 1934

Poor Jelly, my most faithful companion
is a wild animal.

WALLY LAIRD, 1934

As Special Constable I'm the one they call
when there are bear problems around Waskesiu
or Prince Albert. But more often than not,
I'm called for all kinds of other reasons.
I suppose you could say Grey Owl is one
of those reasons. There's a family of foxes
I've taken to feeding, cute little critters.
Grey Owl knows this and has taken a liking to me
because of it. Good by me, he's a nice enough guy
when he's sober
and sure as hell smarter than the lot around here.
Says his father was a McNeil, a Scotsman like me.
One thing for sure, he's well acquainted
with those famous scotch brothers
Blackie and Johnny Red Walker.

GREY OWL, 1934

The bears come snooping around for a snack
and will eat just about anything, honey, shanks of ham,
pails of sugar, garbage.
Can't make a habit of feeding them,
or letting them find food, or else
they become nuisances, real pests,
even though they know better.

This is Wally talking, with sidelong glances at me,
as we drink tea
and smoke our pipes on the porch of his cabin.

He's the RCMP's special constable-interpreter-guide
all rolled into one,
the one who's helped me more than once
get back to the Park. After
I've landed hard
from another bout with myself
all over town.

Olga Pavlova, 1935

One afternoon this tall Indian comes into the store, Simpson's
women's department, where I work during the day, and asks me
if I'm Olga Pavlova. There are all kinds of Indians in Regina
but never in my life have I seen one like him before, very tidy,
very clean, very you know... At first I don't know if I should
speak to him, until he introduces himself, then of course
I recognize immediately who he is, who wouldn't?

He tells me he's a big fan of mine. He listens to me
sing on the radio and he is happy to see I'm as pretty
as he imagined. I likewise compliment him. He's not so bad
looking himself. After that we go out to dinner whenever
he's in town.

He even writes and asks if I would consider becoming his
secretary and going on a tour of Britain with him.
He says I would be perfect and imagines me on a darkened stage,
dressed in a white gown lit by a spotlight, singing a classical
prelude to his entrance. I answer I'd love to, but I can't.
I'm still married. He's disappointed, but we remain friends.

Archie Belaney, Notebook, 1935

There are more orders from publishers than I can possibly fill.
I have already turned down 24 articles for British magazines,
plus 6 for Canadian. I wish I had someone to advise me.
It's bewildering.

JOURNEY

Lovat Dickson, 1935

He arrives in rain. I hurry him
        into the car and we're off
towards London. At first sight, tall,
        lithe and powerful,
he's everything I could have ever
        hoped for and more, much:
black hat, black hair, black suit, red
        handkerchief, moccasins
— the look of a wildwest preacher.
        Perfect.

It's dark and we're in a rush so I
        don't notice right away,
but only later when we arrive
        at the hotel, the most peculiar
and startling feature about him. His
        eyes, they're rivetting,
two blue bird's eggs against skin of
        autumn bark;
the effect is the mark of a visionary
        or a fanatic.

GREY OWL, 1935

The hotel turns out to be all that I dread, the epitome
of Victorian respectability heavy with priggish gloom.
It's my past waiting to have it out with me. It's the moment
I enter and know I can't spend the night here.
But arrangements have been made, and I'm checked in
and escorted up the narrow stairway.
I'm about to say I must go elsewhere, but where?
And besides what's the use, the next would be the same,
and so instead I tell myself to calm down
and hold on, clutch the banister, as I make my way up
twenty creaking stairs. I've no choice
but to think this through. Through the nauseating smell
of old chamber pots and cigar smoke.
When we arrive at my room, he opens the door
and invites me to go ahead in.

Sleep well.

I'll come by in the morning, and we can have breakfast
and go over the itinerary. Our first engagement
is the press conference at ten.
Fine, I say.
Well good-night, he says, finality in his voice,
and closes the door behind him.

Listen.

Immediately I wrench open the only window. The room is a box,
the walls a pattern of musty flowers, the bed purple velvet.
I've been here before. That must be it. The moment I entered
I could've sworn I had stayed here years ago — maybe as a child
with my grandmother when we came to London to visit Ivy
and her mother? Ivy, my dearly departed wife. Are you still
at Bayswater? Are you still waiting for your husband to return?
He said he would. What difference does it make? That past
is dead. Bury it. Let it rest in peace.
That was someone else, some Englishman named Belaney
who died and was reborn. Grey Owl. A name I've earned,

which no one can take away from me. I don't need her, or
anyone to tell me who I am. The Indians know. Alex knows.
I have no need to defend myself. My work speaks for itself.

Hear Me.

I know what this room is, it's a coffin. It's Archibald do this,
Archibald do that. It's everything I've ever wanted to escape,
and here I am, back, shut in for the night, in a hotel — no,
a mausoleum — where elderly ladies, like Aunt Ada and Carrie,
might stay. Or where those sorrowful excuses, stuffed
into a collar and tie, might come with their women of leisure,
where the good gentleman won't be recognized. Why am I here?
Why was I brought here to England? There must be a reason.
Is it to show me where I belong? Well I don't belong,
not any more. To show me what it's like to die
stifled in such a room? And I won't be trapped, not here,
never. It's too late for that. I'm already bound to my purpose.
Steel teeth have already snapped into my flesh and spirit
— for if I am trapped then I have already trapped myself.

Get out.

I need a drink. In my packsack there's a bottle. Dig it out.
Make sure to re-tie the straps in case I have to leave
in a hurry. Pour a shot into the glass on the table. Drink.
Pour another. Drink more. And another. One more. Yes,
tomorrow when they come to pick me up they will be surprised
to see that I haven't slept, but I can't risk sleep,
give this place a chance to slit me open like an eye
and steal inside. Let this room pull out exhibits
from the back of my mind, old photographs of me posing stiffly
beside my Aunt's dog or in my little sailor suit, evidence
of who I'm supposed to be. I can hear the whispers,
the murmur of dead wood (Is someone on the stairs?)
or dead people, demanding proper answers for my behaviour.

Go Back.

Beside the window is a desk. I've got pen and paper. My only hope is to write myself out of here. Tonight, get back north, get past this walled-in death as fast as I can and return home to my beaver, to the wind in the trees and all the other voices of the woodlands who have accepted me without reserve or judgement. Where I can listen and wonder, and explain my side of my life without my every word and action scrutinized by a pack of non-believing skeptics, who want truth no more than a wolf wants bread. Where I can breathe easily and freely. Yes, I must try to breathe and relax, think of those who have made me what I am. Yes.

Feel north.

LOVAT DICKSON, 1935

When I opened his door next morning he was standing
exactly where I left him ten hours before.
His pack still lay on the bed. The straps
hadn't been undone, or his bed slept in.
I could not believe that he had stood there all night,
but I had to believe it. His face was white
and strained. Without any other greeting,
he said to me in a low tense voice,
Get me out of here, brother.

WA-SHA-QUON-ASIN
HE WHO WALKS BY NIGHT

Because you must
  There's no one else
  You're the first
    The vanguard
You're the trail itself

Night is forever
It's a feeling
  vast as Lake Biscotasing
    high as a white pine
It's a moon that cares for you
Stars that escort you
Beasts that watch
  It's the edge
the private

At night the wind feigns sleep
  You hear the slightest stirring
    Everything is something else
Everything is free
Anything can happen

GREY OWL, 1935

Have you heard the one about the Indian and the Ambassador?
Upon being introduced the Indian simply said hello.
The Ambassador was shocked to hear such a greeting
coming from an Indian and asked:
Aren't you people supposed to say HOW?
We know how, responded the Indian.
All we want is a chance.

***

The Times calls me a new Canadian Ambassador.
I become the talk of London and get invited
here, there, everywhere: At Foyle's Literary Luncheon
five hundred people crowd in to hear me,
the famous and sometimes infamous (pardon me),
writers and adventurers,
Sirs and Lords; they in their tails, me in my buckskin;
everybody looking intensely interested
or absolutely bored
                    for the cameras.
Fascinating.
Marvelous.
Simply divine. I hear them say, as they sip ever so daintily
on their second, third — oh, who's counting — aperitif.

As for me, they try to head me off at the pass
(an old Buffalo Bill expression from my youth, I dare say)
and make sure to serve me plenty of tea.
Got to keep the Indian away from the firewater,
I see the waiters smirk.
Little do they know that I know
exactly
their kind. So what do I do? Play along,
of course. I hold on tight to my Hudson Bay blanket,
come on wise and witty,
and do my best to keep a straight face.

A body could get used to such a life, soft
and bloated white,
as for the mind, that's another matter; after a month
mine is crawling the walls black: Am I? Am I? Am I?
                    Contradicting myself.
And with three more
months to go.

GREY OWL, 1935

You in the audience who sit in expectation cannot know.

This fear, this inexorable fear, I take with me,
so much a part of me I carry it in my blood. Picture me
stepping onto the stage and into a beam of light.
I look out to the audience, to you,
but I see only a curtain of black. Certainly I hear
your applause, the rumble of voices, the clapping of hands,
and I greet this not without a small degree of satisfaction,
but I am far from at ease (though this air I try to assume)
as I make my way to the podium, for here darkness is no forest
sanctuary but more a murky abyss, ready to open greedily
like the mouth that it is, with a sharp, accusing shriek.

The music has come to an end: Beethoven's "Moonlight Sonata,"
an echo of my childhood, of Highbury Villa, of Aunt Ada
towering over me, a music that continues to swell my past
inside me but which for some unknown reason — Call it love
— I continue to use as a prelude to my entrance.

Call it affliction.

The film is rolling; no, correction, I haven't yet given the cue.
After a prefatory greeting in which I tell you I come in peace,
I'm now launched into a story of my early days as a riverman,
or maybe I'm mentioning how different it was for me to move
to northern Ontario from the southern United States, to learn
the still-hunt of the Ojibway as compared to the whoop
and holler of the Apache buffalo hunt.

What I do know is that I'm in the middle of a sentence when
as though by lightning my words are struck down.
Without warning. From behind the black curtain
where you sit, someone is shouting: Liar! Liar!

Nothing but a liar.

Immediately the house lights come on with a hush as blinding
and as penetrating as the darkness which has now accumulated
in the person of the woman who stands in front of me
dressed in black with a veil masking her face,
as though she were in mourning. Is she?

All heads are turned towards her,
as she extends her arm and points to me.
You and the rest of the audience are aghast, struck dumb.
No one knows what to do. In the room's startled breath,
you could hear a leaf drop, except there are no leaves,
for this is a London auditorium, no leaves, no trees,
no place to hide.

The woman is now addressing those seated around her.
She tells you that she knows me.
Her? Me? Yes, me. She slowly nods,
as she raises her veil and looks me in the eye.
She is close, so close I can see the tears,
the torn smile, her emotions mixed and ravenous,
as she fulfills her dream come true of confronting me.

He's both a liar and a scoundrel.
I know, I'm his wife. Here, look! She screams,
and raises her left hand to show off a wedding ring,
and then from her handbag pulls out a couple of photographs:
Ask him about these, she says amid the flashing cameras
to the photographers who have managed to shove their way
towards her, while two ushers try to grab hold of her.

But the audience is calling for her to continue.
Continue. And so she gives them dates and names,
the name of the church, the presiding minister,
witnesses, guests, and on and on.
It turns out she is not alone.
One by one others in the audience begin to stand,
begin to make their way towards me, all
bearing an accusing finger.

And you, whoever you are, are swept up among them.
Before I can even get off stage, find a way to escape,
you have all encircled me and together
are pointing and chanting in unison:
Archibald, Archibald Stansfeld Belaney.
The photographers have also surrounded me, flashbulbs
explode in my face. Blinded. There is no escape.

The haunted has become the hunted.

I press my hands to my ears and implore everyone to stop,
to let me go: for you know now who I am.
Helpless, I fall to my knees. And above me, there she is,
Ivy, the young actress Belaney once loved and abandoned.
And beside her, all his old Hastings Grammar School classmates
laughing at odd-ball Archie who's still playing Indian
after all these years.

GREY OWL, 1935-36

Why have you come? the reporters ask
as they jostle for position,
try to get me to crack my grimace
for the flashing cameras.
To offer hope, I announce.
I come bearing a green leaf.
I come to speak to your tired and
factory beaten, to the colliers
with their coal-blackened eyes.
To say that you too can find refuge
beyond the smokestacks,
the daily toil of your civilization,
and escape to a place of peace
and contentment.

I speak of life, of the animals
great and small, and of the land
we share in harmony across the ocean.
For it too is now threatened,
overwhelmed by the hungry maw
you all know so well. But hark!
I exclaim. All is not lost.
Recognize that what has been forsaken
by your forefathers exists,
here in my words,
in my books and films,
for I am the Voice of Nature.

Lovat Dickson, 1936

He's lecturing to packed halls every night,
so by now he's more or less wealthy.
I haven't given him his share yet — I'm afraid to
but make sure to keep him in spending money, enough
to let him buy whatever catches his fancy.
He has good taste and buys the finest, some
real antiques,
like the brass tomahawk with the inlaid handle
or the bear claw necklace.   (Some
                                of it, mind you,
                                like the eagle feather
                                headdress, is not old at all
                                but merely expensive.)

When he has it he spends it, but not always.
Because the moment he sees a vagrant on the street,
he's ready to empty his pockets. In fact, he does
exactly that a number of times, before we stop him
and explain that he must try to act more civilized.

Archie Belaney, Notebook, 1935

Money? Jobs? Progress?

What's life without Nature?
Wildlife? Solitude?

But two hands wrapped around
your throat.

One of the most romantic figures ever to visit England
will be in Leeds. Grey Owl is his name, a Canadian Indian
who has just arrived in this country for a three month's lecture
tour. A pilgrimage is what Grey Owl calls it — a pilgrimage
undertaken on behalf of his people and the small creatures
of the forests with whom he has identified himself so closely.

THE LONDON TIMES, NOVEMBER 2, 1935

A picturesque figure in Indian dress, with the thoughtful face
of a philosopher, Grey Owl comes as a friend of nature.

I break the silence of many years to tell things that have been
hidden for a long time in the shadowy forests of the Canadian
wilds, he said yesterday. I am an ambassador from the wild
lands, an interpreter of the little brothers of the wilds.
I am trying to lay a foundation on which abler and better hands
will later build.

HARROGATE HERALD, NOVEMBER 13, 1935

Struggle to Enter — There were busy scenes outside the Royal
Hall on Monday evening. So large was the number of people
wishing to gain admission to the Literary Society for the lecture
by the famous Red Indian author and naturalist, Grey Owl,
that five minutes to eight, ticket holders were still in the
growing queue. Waving their tickets, they began a frenzied
attempt to get in and eventually a side door was thrust open,
much against the remonstrances of an attendant.

NOTTINGHAM JOURNAL & EXPRESS, NOVEMBER 20, 1935

A very remarkable man is in Nottingham this week.
You can see him and hear him, at the Albert Hall, tomorrow,
if you wish to have an experience that you will remember
for a long time. This is Grey Owl, half-primitive, half-complex...
the modern, the literary, Hiawatha.

ROMANTIC

James Fenimore Cooper,
why, yes, I've read him.
  Last of the Mohicans
  Deerslayer etc. etc.
Fine books. Fine books indeed.

Certainly they're romanticized,
but then, it's all part of the game,
isn't it? To give the public
what it wants,
& expects.

I say if they want romance
                    give it to them.
If they expect beads and braids
                    give it to them.
Butter the facts.
Spread it thick.
The point is
to get the message
across,
isn't it?

GEOFFREY TURNER, 1936

As a student of the North American Indian and Associate
of the Department of Ethnology and Prehistory, University
of Oxford, I have, as you can appreciate, a professional interest in
this Grey Owl, and, accordingly, I make certain to arrive
at the theatre in plenty of time to get a good seat.

It's a January evening, and I've had to travel across London;
my mood of expectation thus already miserably dampened
soon gives way to exasperation, when I see this chap who claims
to be part Apache, adopted by the Ojibway, tread to centre stage
— as though walking on eggs — only to raise his arm and greet
the audience with "How Kola," an expression undoubtedly Sioux,
and with a beam of light focused ever so dramatically
on his stiff scowling face.

Clearly a showman if there ever was one, all style and no
substance, straight from the pages of Longfellow, Hiawatha
in person. Squirming in my seat, I don't know whether to leave
and disturb those sitting beside me, or stay and see this
character through. But before I've decided my initial despair
vanishes in awe — against his overwrought introduction, he
now projects candor and humour. For on a screen behind him
are two beaver actually building a lodge inside his cabin.

You should've seen the branch I made Jelly Roll leave outside,
he says to the laughing crowd, of the beaver now shown
trying to wedge half a tree in through the door. Then, an image
of this strange man himself, holding up a chair with one leg
chewed off, a shovel with only part of a handle, pointing
to the teeth marks around the room. This is what I've come for,
I have to admit, the real stuff. Certainly no cigarstore wooden
Indian here.

QUESTION/ ANSWER

The question is whether
or not.

What do I see?
      What do you?
            Do we see the same?
                 (How can we?)

So I stand and speak.
I have no choice.
I cannot live with what I see.

What choice is there anyway?
Do we choose birth
parents
home
sight?
Do we choose time?

The time it takes.
Enough to try
at least
to answer.

LOVAT DICKSON, 1936

A couple of brisk knocks and he hollers to come in.
After more than a hundred performances the strain
is setting in on all of us, but still I'm surprised
to notice the skin of his face stretched tight
as the sheet of the bed he invites me to sit on.
He's occupying the only chair, sitting next to a dressing table,
and as he pulls his eyes towards me, away from the bottle
of Dewar's he has been working on, he raises his glass
and asks me to join him. I have no idea where he got the liquor
as I'm doing my best to curtail his drinking by providing
as little opportunity as possible. (Probably from
someone engaged in the hotel, I suspect). He notices
my disapproval and with a sigh says a drink is exactly
what he needs. I can see he's in no mood to be told
what he can and cannot do. All the same,
it is high time we had a talk.

I accept his offer and, while he's pouring, I tell him the reason
I knocked is to bring to his attention yet another invitation
to dine with the social prominent, the elite,
and that it would be a good idea to accept as selected members
of the press will also be in attendance. As usual,
he says to do what I think is best
and make whatever arrangements necessary, although tonight
he is uncommonly talkative. He appears to need company.
Another drink and a wilderness of memory is in the room
with us, a lament tolling in his voice,
as he tells me about his beaver. Clearly he misses them.
To him they are the happy times
and their well-being his greatest concern.
We have known one another for a mere three months,
the time we've spent motoring throughout Britain,
and so he describes at length his life in Canada
and, in particular, how Jelly Roll and Rawhide
have brought so much change to it.

He says nothing of Anahareo. And that's when it strikes me
that the heroine of his story, this leading lady
with the madonna-like smile, whom we see on screen

cradling one of the beaver, feeding a fox, holding
out a hand to a whiskeyjack, may be in reality
a product of Grey Owl's own imagination,
in other words, his own creation, which may not
have anything to do with the flesh and blood
of the woman. This I wonder, as he takes up the bottle
to offer me a refill, and I unwittingly plunge
into asking about her. He doesn't say much, only
that she is at the lodge taking care of the beaver.
Then, before I can comment further, he rises and
says it's getting late and we have a full day tomorrow,
which surprises me coming from a man who pays little
or no regard to time.

Before I leave there is still something that must be brought
into the open. But how to forge the flood of nervous silence
into which each utterance wants to slip? It's then
that I too stand, but instead of following him to the door,
I take up the bottle, and as though examining the label
casually mention that I hope he'll save some for tomorrow.
Quickly he swings around, mindful of what I'm getting at.
And I add that there's still a lot of work ahead for us,
another heavy month of miles to go and halls to stump,
and we mustn't forget the public has a certain expectation.
We have created a certain image which must be maintained.
Therefore, whatever problem any of us might have
must be kept under control and out of sight,
whether it be homesickness, a case of nerves,
or this, I say, clasping and shaking the bottle.
I look away, so as not to feel his steely gaze, and finish
by saying that I hope he understands. He doesn't answer.
On my way out I close the door quietly behind me,
still wondering about the woman.

ARCHIE BELANEY, 1936

Insurmountable wall I never overcome,
which exists really only in imagination
until at last discover no wall, too late.

You Ask

What it's like to see your EX-wife up on the screen,
the woman you haven't lived with in years looking
like the first day of your lives together
— and the last — like cherry pie and blood,
as she cradles a beaver kitten in her arms
while the audience Ahhhhs and Woooos.

Keep face. Keep face. Face her. Face them. The truth?

It leaves a stone in your throat that sinks to your heart
because what you feel is thick and heavy. Because she's part
of the fiction, and they ask continuously about her
and you clamp your red teeth and say she's at home
and everything is w-o-n-d-e-r-f-u-l, b-l-i-s-s-f-u-l,
grass grows green, birds sing daily.

What's it like to have to keep this sticky poise
performance after performance, all two hundred and twenty?
When your mind regurgitates every moment you've spent with her,
re-memorizes every embrace, re-reads every word
you've ever written to her — aloud,
clamorous — for only yourself to hear.

Dear. Dearest.

I think I'm losing it. You. Your love. Myself. Yes,
most surely I've lost myself, to this man I've become,
this man I am, to this work I've taken on, to the public,
the people who think they know me but don't understand and
never will. My body, my spirit one with this trail or trial
or whatever you want to call it.

My Pony. My Gertie. My Anahareo.

Sorry for having been cross with you, for carrying on
the way I did, when I know that I may never see you again,
except on the screen, forever untouchable and cold
as the silver image you are up there. Please try
and forget, and forgive if you can.

LOVAT DICKSON, 1935-36

As his publisher my idea was to bring him to Britain
on a speaking tour, set up a number of engagements
in public halls, and just maybe there would be enough interest
to cover expenses and generate sales of his latest two books.
A risk beyond compare, and I was prepared to appeal
to church groups and even the Boy Scouts, if I had to.
To say I was singularly naive would be a generous
understatement. Naivety reigns. The public pounces on him.
And Grey Owl, the wise old bird, invites us all to feast,
takes us all under his wing.

Both books are reprinted, *Pilgrims of the Wild* five times,
Sajo and The Beaver People four. We're selling five thousand
copies of each a month. The halls are filled to capacity,
often 3 times a day. In Glasgow 3,000 people turn up,
that same evening he leaves for Canterbury and travels more
than 300 miles by car, lecturing non-stop along the way.
In four months he gives over 200 lectures, addresses 250,000 people,
months of rushing from city to city, hotel to hotel, lecture
to lecture.

By the time we put him back on board a ship for Canada,
he's about to collapse. He has neither missed a single lecture,
nor mentioned money. When I hand him over his half-share
of receipts, his face, already drawn out of shape, goes white
as paper, from a wilderness man to a rich man almost overnight.
For him money means one thing, more opportunity to spread his
message, a tour of Canada and the U.S.A. and then back to Britain
with a new book and new films. The cameras are already rolling
inside him, and he's off shooting rapids on the North Atlantic.

After four months of lectures, he's so exhausted, both mentally
and physically, we picture him walking into walls or falling
overboard or giving away all his money, which he loves to do
anyway. And so I agree to escort him back to Canada.
He's arrived with one packsack and returns with eight trunks
of gifts lavished on him and Anahareo by admiring fans,
everything from Royal Doulton china to books signed
by their authors. But it's the two items he's bought
for himself that he cherishes above all else. The first
is a portable gramophone, which includes a stack of classical
records — everything from Beethoven to Tchaikovsky. (He,
in fact, uses the press clippings to pack the records.)
The second is a magnificent eagle feather warbonnet
of white plumage trimmed with red brocade, bought
in a novelty shop on Picadilly.

As for the bonnet, it proves to be worse than a newborn babe.
Fearing the trunk will crush its delicate down, he takes it
in his arms as soon as he can and cradles it. On the train
to Greenock, from where we are to sail, this huge thing
occupies nearly all the space of the compartment. Feathers
in my face — and me with my allergies. He also insists
we ride with the window open in order to give it plenty
of air. Fine, but it happens to be February.
As for the music, it becomes a means of diversion and so,
during the first couple of weeks of our trans-Atlantic voyage,
I sit on the floor of his cabin constantly winding up the
gramophone, playing it non-stop
from 8 A.M. to midnight, to the point where
I'm craving peace and quiet. And yet all things considered,
I have little choice; I know what will happen
if I leave him alone:

He looks ill.
When he tries on the headdress
the pale feathers match the colour of his skin.
I also notice his breath smells of onion
(it's all he appears to be eating),

and I suppose he's taking some kind of Indian remedy.
Until, one stormy afternoon, out from under the bed
comes rolling three empty whiskey bottles.

Exasperated, on my hands and knees
with the gramophone, I rip off the record,
jump to my feet and call him a fake.
He, stunned, turns even whiter
than he is, and timidly apologizes
promising to stop.

Five days out of Halifax, he's eating again and now begins
to work on a new book he'll call *Tales Of An Empty Cabin.*
I agree to take on the job of secretary and take notes
while he dictates. First thing I know, he's going at it full steam
ahead — as though his life depended on it, and I'm up all night
scribbling as fast as I can. The cabin hot and stuffy, filled
with smoke from his black cigarillos. All I want to do is go
to my own cabin and sleep and all he wants to do is work.
OK, another hour, I say, but that's it.
I've got to go to bed... but how can I even think of sleep
when waves of inspiration slap through him, and he's bolt upright
in his chair talking as though he was there, back somewhere
out there, and I'm fascinated and don't want to be the one
responsible for extinguishing the wave, the burning wave.
Six o'clock in the morning and he finally comes to a halt
and says it's going to be a glorious day,
so why don't we see if we can get a coffee and go on deck
and watch the sunrise fill the ocean. And I look out
and it's true, soon everything will be glowing crimson,
and lying on the bed are thirty pages, and it feels so good
to see them that I agree with him
even in my exhaustion.

HUGH EAYRS, 1936

As his Canadian publisher I escort him to various meetings
we have arranged for him in Toronto. What immediately
becomes evident is that he is quite scared of meeting people.
He gives us the distinct impression of being actually frightened,
which has been plain to see on numerous occasions.

Grey Owl, 1936

Eayrs asks if I'm uncomfortable with Toronto because it conjures
up old associations for me. That's not it at all, I explain.
After my tour of Britain I'm like a river with no water. And
what I say is true. I am drained. Besides, how can I tell him
that behind my eyes there is a crowd and in that crowd a face,
any number of faces.

Hi Archie, remember me? he or she asks.
No, I answer.
Sure you do, don't be frightened Archie.

It's me Bill Guppy, remember, I gave you your first job,
    when you looked like you'd just got off the boat.
It's me Angele, your wife. I married you in Temegami.
    You had soft skin and made good love.
It's me Harry, Harry Woods, the Hudson Bay's post manager
    at Temegami. I remember you, the young greenhorn
    eager to learn Indian.
It's me Marie. Remember our winter together in the bush?
    We had fun didn't we Archie?
Archie it's me Quill, I taught you how to handle a canoe
    when you didn't know one end of the paddle
    from the other.
It's me Tom, Tom Saville, I was best man at your wedding
    in Temegami. She misses you, you know.
It's me John Egwuna. It's not a good thing what you did
    to my niece Archie. We gave you our trust.
Belaney, you rogue, it's me J.J. O'Connor, the lawyer
    who served you your English wife's divorce papers.
    What was her name?
It's me Archie, George McCormick, your Hastings school pal.
    Boy, do you look different.
Archibald Belaney. You don't know me, but I'm your cousin
    Maggie. Your aunts wrote me you were in Canada.

Christianity Unsuited For Indians
Famous Red Man Thinks
                                    —*Toronto Star, 1936*

GREY OWL, 1936

In Toronto I make a mistake. I tell the press what I think
about organized religion, and I awake to glaring headlines
and a blaring telephone. Reporters wanting more interviews.
Ministers wanting me to repent. Crank callers wanting me
to get out of town.

Among other things that stampede out of me, I say
that in this world we are all travelling one great trail
towards one great end. And that all religions
preach the great fundamental truths, which if properly
understood, would all confer great benefits on a struggling,
bewildered humanity.

I say that if missionaries want to do good, their first duty
towards the Indian should be to give him the means to live
in a changing world, give him employment and self-sufficiency,
so that he may once again raise his head with dignity.
Besides, is it not difficult to teach Christianity
to someone with an empty belly?

Tolerance, I say. For us, the forest and all the works of God
have a soul and must be treated as such, with respect.
Yet, in my meagre research I have failed to find in Christianity
any emphasis on tolerance to what is known as the lower forms
of life. Is it not sad to see all the countless good people
scrambling to provide themselves with safe passage
to the hereafter while treating the rest of creation
with disdain?

What I find strange is that we are told to accept
another man's interpretation of the world and life when
we have our own. Does not the old Indian faith teach honesty,
integrity, reverence, love of nature and love of fellow man?

What is more, it is a faith filled with music, dance
and poetic beauty.

Speaking as a pagan, I tell them I must say what I believe.
To the Indian, those who still practice the ancient rites,
prayer has never become the servile supplication
it has for the whiteman. I say this — you might say
I'm throwing fat on the fire — and the first thing I know
the city is up in arms. And I admit, it's kind of nice
to see all those white collars get a little sweaty.

ARCHIE BELANEY, NOTEBOOK, 1936

I don't have to preach to the Indian. They knew conservation
before I was born or my father before me. They don't need me,
unless it is the civilized halfbreeds and Indians
who have gone white.

Donalda Legace, 1936

I can't believe it. Here I am, me, in my dream house,
sitting on the most comfortable sofa I could ever imagine,
my hand resting on the rich fabric, surrounded by walnut
furniture, silk drapes, paintings, books, music. Wine served
in crystal. And it all belongs to one of Archie's friends.
Pinch me and I'll scream not to wake up.

He asks me how long I intend to be in Toronto and I tell him
me and my husband got to be getting back north tomorrow.
But we saw his picture and where he was staying in the
newspaper — I already cut out the article for a souvenir —
and decided to see if he had time for an old Bisco friend.
You weren't much more than a teenager when I left, he says.
Twenty-three, I say. It's been eleven years.
I surprise him when I tell him this
because for a moment he looks past me like he's confused
until he shakes away whatever he sees.

He's eager to know everything: so I tell him my mother died
and someone else is now running the boarding house.
That Alex Espaniel hasn't been feeling too well. About
Ted Cusson. Jack Leve. All the bits and pieces
of gossip I've picked up over the years.

Archie Belaney in the flesh. Or rather in a fancy red shirt.
He looks pretty much the same, at least the way I remember him.
Maybe a little thinner, certainly older, maybe more Indian
looking, but the same good-natured crazy-wild guy who'd tease
the girls then buy them sweets from the Hudson Bay store. Always
going on about something: like now. Yeah. That's just the way
it happened, I nod like a good little girl, like I was back
in school, making it sound like he's the hero or culprit
of every story. Yeah it was you
who chopped the posts under the dance hall
so they'd give way the moment the dancing
got going. Yeah it was you
who tied up the teacher as if you
were going to scalp her.

Archie always loved the limelight,
and I can't say he's changed
one single teeny-weeny bit.

One day, and I'm sure that day will come,
when they ask me what I think about Archie Belaney Grey Owl,
I'll say what they'll never expect to hear.
Simply that he was the best thing that ever happened to me.
He was the only time
I ever got to see my dream come true.

Morning After, Toronto, 1936

After the kisses
and handshakes,
the party's over
and the past goes home
with the visitors.

At least you expect it to.

What's it like to sit up all night
with wives
dead
or as good as dead,
each one taking her turn?

To emerge from your den
(of books? of leaves?)
pierced yellow eyes
stabbed by daylight,
eyes caught
oozing memory.

What's it like?
It's like fire
or firewater, in your mouth
while you are trying to explain.
It's like death — that's it,
to talk to the dead.

GREY OWL, 1936

Seven o'clock, a cement grey mid-March morning.
I'm sitting in a small café, a stone's throw from Parliament,
having a cup of coffee while the Chinese owner
wipes the counter-top. A small chime hooked to the door rings
but I don't pay it any mind. Today I'm meeting the Governor
General, Lord Tweedsmuir, tomorrow Mackenzie King himself.
I'm hoping they'll agree to government funding for the films
I want to make on the Mississauga River. When I finally look up
from the newspaper headline — Hitler Invades Rhineland —
which I realize I've been staring at blankly, there seated
at the end of an empty row of red vinyl stools is a young Indian,
who in contrast to my buckskin is wearing a dark overcoat and
tie. A knapsack lies at his feet.

To me he looks lost, uncertain where exactly he is,
so I hold up my hand and say, Hey brother mind if I join you?
He immediately recognizes me (no doubt from my pictures
in the newspapers). It turns out to be John Tootoosis' first time
in Ottawa. He's just arrived by train from Saskatchewan
to present the resolutions of the League of Indians
of Western Canada to officials from the Department
of Indian Affairs. He doesn't have a place to stay yet
so I invite him back to the Plaza Hotel. Plenty of room,
I insist, more room than my cabin out on Lake Ajawaan,
besides I've got a full day ahead of me anyway. You can rest
and then see about getting a room for yourself. He agrees,
and I bring him back to the hotel. We make arrangements to meet
later that evening.

Over supper, he explains the present situation of his people
in western Canada. Although I, myself, live in Saskatchewan
I've had little contact with the local Indians and know
little of their history. He tells me that Chief Poundmaker,
his great uncle, took sides with Louis Riel,
in what John calls the Great Resistance of 1885,
and ever since then the government has come down hard
as steel fencing and has taken all control away.

He insists that we Indian people cannot continue to exist
without control of our own destiny. No people can.
For me his words are like water bubbling around my head,
I hear things I never dreamed of hearing.
This is a new dream, his dream,
and I've been allowed inside.

I tell him that I've witnessed the destitution
among the Indians of northern Ontario, families without
money to buy flour because the government built a railroad
through their traditional lands, their only compensation
the influx of white trappers who kill everything in sight.
Tell him I've witnessed the deaf-eared, iron-fisted
government policy which has turned a once-independent people
into vagrants dependent upon hand-outs and at the mercy
of some self-righteous Indian Agent. But John,
I exclaim, this is the first time I've ever heard
about Indian people coming together and actually trying
to do something about their situation.
There is no going back, he says.

And I feel it's as though I've been living in darkness,
my head only now just broken to the lighted surface.
These are not the Indians the British public wants to see.
Not the Indian I represent. No tomahawks and fancy riding.
I want him to go on, and he speaks intensely with a voice
that rises and soars like those of old, but his is not old
— it's new and tells me he is not alone but one of many —
and I listen all night and into the early hours of the morning.
When we finally say good-night or rather good-morning (and
laugh), I can't help but wonder that of all the restaurants
in Ottawa, why did we happen to walk into the same one
at the same unlikely hour?

But it's obvious that this young man was meant
to walk into Wong's Café while I was there, the two of us
alone, pulled in together by the light — a sign

meant to be. He was meant to come in and give me direction,
inform me of my next move, just as I was meant to listen.
The next day I tell him that I've got a few connections,
and I'll see what I can do to further the cause.
I can't promise anything. To begin with though
I can at least accompany him to the Department
of Indian Affairs so that he can be properly
introduced.

JOHN TOOTOOSIS, 1936

An Indian can tell who's Indian.
Grey Owl can't sing or dance.
But he's doing good
and when we meet
I call him Brother.

GREY OWL, 1936

In Ottawa I dine with the Prime Minister
at Laurier House, a draped cavern of candlelight
and crystal, paneled with dark portraits, stern faces
that seem to suck the flickering light from the room
as they stare ominously over my shoulder. Yet,
despite the gloom, the blinding shadow, the stuffy air
of secrecy, King appears genuinely interested in my proposal,
his massive girth shaking hospitably as if he were Santa Claus
himself, as he leans forward at his end of the table
and asks in a tone of receptive confidentiality
to explain exactly what I have in mind.

He asks and I bare my heart and tell him about my plan,
my cherished dream to preserve the Mississauga River
on film, and that with this historical document
of ancient trails and talking waters, I would travel
as a representative of Indian people,
my people,
throughout Great Britain and America
promoting conservation.

Remember, it is you who were instrumental
in turning Prince Albert into a National Park.
This would be another feather in your bonnet.
It's an opportunity that shouldn't be missed,
one that wouldn't take much money.
He professes to like the idea and even raises a toast to it,
but says it is not up to him to make the final decision.
All he can do is recommend it to Crerar, the Minister
of the Interior. All I can do is wait.

Is wait. wait. wait. wait. wait. wait.

I decide to stay in Ottawa and make the rounds of Parliament
trying to meet as many Ministers as possible in hope
of getting them on side. Each day

I also call Crerar's office
and each day I get the same response, no decision
has yet been made. And then one afternoon after
another telephone call and another faceless delay,
I find myself walking into the hotel's bar
to have just one drink.

JOE HASSRAK

One thing about being a bartender, you see everything.

Yeah, he's here drinking at the Plaza hotel, perched
on a bar stool as though this is where he belongs.
Sure he's loud, and I do my best to try and calm him down,
ply him with more drinks (I know it's foolish of me).
Normally we don't even let Indians in, but seeing he's famous
and judging from the looks of him,
he's obviously got a lot of whiteman in him.
So I look the other way, so to speak. Besides,
he's a likeable guy, though certainly a helleva strange bird
in his dark suit, red neckband, hat pulled low.
A heck of a storyteller too.

Right now he's going on about some party he's supposed to be at.
Earlier in the day, he had his photograph taken by Mr. Karsh,
you know the guy who takes pictures of Kings
and Prime Ministers and the like. He says he was invited
back for a dinner in his honour. Mr. Karsh assured him
he would make all the necessary arrangements,
even refurbish his studio to make it look presentable
(imagine that!), order food and wine,
and invite forty or so prominent writers, journalists
and politicians. And now Grey Owl decides
he doesn't want to go. Just like that!
(Maybe there's more Indian in him than I think.)

Anybody who's somebody must be there, eager
to meet the famous Canadian celebrity extraordinaire.
They've all read about him, news of his British tour
has been quick to reach Ottawa. So there they are waiting,
waiting, until their patience is burnt through and
the anxious murmuring in the room has become unbearable
for the host. While Grey Owl sits here in my bar,
at the appointed hour, as though he couldn't care less,
carrying on about something or other, his glass raised,
his voice boisterous.

What is it he's going on about? Something about Indians?
the government? his film? his wife? Something
about himself? career? health? happiness?
That he doesn't care.
And as if that weren't enough, it's exactly at this moment
that I see him, Mr. Karsh, himself.
But rather than approach, he remains at the entrance door
carefully considering what he is witnessing,
as though he were about to take the perfect photograph,
a portrait that tells him he should have known better.

It's been too long and too many portages, and I'm just too tired.
What am I talking about? I'm telling you that I don't care.
If she wants to go, she can go and never come back;
I don't need her; besides I've met someone else. And I don't care
whether or not I get government support — I'm not blind,
I can see what's going on — with or without them
I'll make my film even if I have to do it alone.

And I sure as hell don't care about all those people waiting
for me at the reception. I'll pour another drink into myself
if I want to. Who are they to me?
The people I care about aren't invited.
Would never get invited. Where are they anyway, what's happened
to all the Rivermen of olden days? That's what I want to know.
Where are they all? Do you hear me? Where?
Somebody tell me... You.

MACKENZIE KING, 1936

Certainly I ask for a report on him. We must know to whom
we are supposedly giving taxpayers' money. In fact, I want
to know all there is about him. The very idea of the Brits
fawning over him like awed children is most interesting,
if not amusing, especially when I detect a certain naivety
in him I can but describe as child-like.

The way he tries to sell me his film project, speaking
with such fervour of his people's traditions, as though
there is really a place for them in a modern Canada.
Crerar, my Minister of the Interior and Superintendent-General
of Indian Affairs, is to contact the Indian agents up north
and uncover what he can about him. There is always something.

As for the funds Grey Owl requires, were it politically astute
to intercede and give my approbation, I would do so without
hesitation. But as the situation is tenuous by its very nature,
this government can hardly afford to put itself into a position
of jeopardy. Imagine what our opponents would do if they heard
I was funding an Indian when so many voters are out of work.

And to think our meeting took place Friday-13, a time of ill omen
for the superstitious. One can never be too careful.

Why I Write

So I can live in the past,
earn a living,
protect the beaver,
publicize conservation,
attract attention,
sell 35,000 copies in 3 months,
give 138 lectures in 88 days,
travel over 4,350 miles,
wear feathers,
wear make-up,
play Indian — no
be Indian,
get to go to pow wows,
get to tour Britain,
meet the King & Queen,
become famous,
become alcoholic,
leave a legacy,
lose a wife,
be lonely.

Why didn't you come right back? You knew I was here waiting.
I had work to do.
Work to do, when I'm stuck here looking after your beaver?
My beaver? I thought they were our beaver.
Once upon a time, maybe.
Look, I was trying to get money for my film.
Another film? That's all I ever hear from you. Got to do this,
     got to that.
Pass me the bottle. I don't have to listen to you.
Don't you think you've had enough?
You'll know when I've had enough.
Archie! Stop it.
You stop it. You're the one always running off half-cocked.
     Why don't you finish something for once? At least I finish
     what I start. What's happened to the money I've dished out
     over the years for all your prospecting schemes? I haven't
     seen any results.
You're not going to start that again. I'll leave.
Leave. That's one thing you're good at. Why are you always
     trying to evade the truth? You leave your daughter
     with Mrs. Winter and take off for who knows how long.
     Did Dawn even recognize you? You don't write — Oh,
     excuse me, once in four months.
Stop it, I said! You have no right to talk to me that way.
     Give me the bottle.
No way.
Give it to me I said.
Try and take it.
OK, if that's what you want. Don't think I can play rough eh?
You think you're tough because you've been on your own. Is
     that it? Well let me tell you something, you're nothing but
     a little girl, little Pony who never grew up.
Oh yeah, and who are you? Someone who doesn't have the guts
     to get out while he still can.
Little Pony who cares for nobody but herself.
Archie stop it, I said.

The most beautiful romances are the unfulfilled;
completed they fall into the realm of the commonplace.

GREY OWL TO LOVAT DICKSON, 1936

I am writing to let you know that I am now free
to continue my interrupted work.
Last week I had my final row with Anahareo
here in Prince Albert, at which time she unsuccessfully
tried for about 40 minutes
to choke me.

Mirror

In the end
there is no escape.
    (Did I say there was?)
It is always me.
No matter what I do
to change
the way I look.
What is inside is inside looking out.

I see it all (home, family, friends, wives...).

Is this the reason
I'm happiest
making miles
in my canoe —
going to beat hell
over the surface of some lake?

I dip my paddle,
pull hard,
the water ripples
and swirls,
for a moment
the mirror
I'm riding
smashed to a million pieces.

BETTY SOMERVELL, 1936

It's November. In the morning I go down to the lake
and break the ice crusted between the cattails and lily pads.
Standing here, shrouded in mist, watching the tardy geese
high overhead, the beaver pushing branches as they prepare
for the onslaught, I think I can understand
what it must be like to be shut in for the winter.

I have come to Beaver Lodge with my husband to spend a week
with Grey Owl before we go back to England. And I find her here,
Anahareo, whom I have heard so much about, but have never met,
until now. Surprised to see her, shocked to see them together,
because although I have seen her on film with the beaver,
I never realized how young she is compared to him.
Next to her, he looks old, and I might even say frail.
Certainly, the rigors of his British tour have exacted a toll,
just yesterday bringing in a couple pails of water
he had to stop and take hold of a tree to catch his breath.
Imagine, a man who's portaged hundred of pounds,
it's hard to believe how his health has so drastically
deteriorated.

They haven't seen one another for at least six months;
yet the warmth between them appears to be touched
with sadness. It's the way they treat one another,
certainly not as lovers, or even man and wife
who have settled into comfortable co-existence; no,
rather they appear as long-time companions, partners
in a relationship in which there has always been inevitable
parting, who together have suffered and endured hunger and
neglect, and not only overcame these and other privations,
but triumphed to find in their midst those little happinesses
money and fame can never buy. Together again,
these are times they re-visit, for it seems to me
theirs is a relationship of memory, linked
like the coming snow, a flurry of greetings
and then a melting away.

While they remain below in the main cabin with the beaver,
we take the upper guest cabin. Over dinner Grey Owl
plays Chopin on his prized gramophone, and goes on about
his plans for another tour of Britain,
about the new films he's determined to make,
even about a historical novel he's got in mind.
All this while she stares at the fire
without saying a word, her face reflected red.
The day before we are to leave, we sit by the shore
to catch the last of the fading sun. Grey Owl uses this time
to go out in his canoe, and I can see it's the one place
where he's his old self, happy
to cut loose across the water.

He's trying to paddle away what I told him last night,
she says unexpectedly, looking up from her steaming cup.
This time I'm leaving for good. See how far he is?
She points to his nearly invisible outline
against the distant shoreline: that's us. I'm here,
he's over there, and we're pointed in different directions.
We visit, but we don't open up. What we do is merely skim
the surface of each other's life and end up sinking
into how it was six-seven years ago. I ask myself
if it's because he's giving so much of himself to his work
he's got nothing left to spare. Well I can't give
without receiving. You heard his plans,
that's his life, not mine. I told him
I'm going to California.

Before rising to go, she asks if she can come with us
to Prince Albert when we leave. Late that night,
I'm awakened by what sounds like an owl hooting.
At the window I notice a lamp still burning
in their cabin. In the morning,
when we go for breakfast, we discover the canoe
already packed and ready. She takes the stern,

and Grey Owl pushes us off. Quickly,
she begins to paddle, vigorously swinging
her shoulders into each smooth stroke,
until her panting breath looks like steam in the brisk air.
Then, as quickly as she began, she stops and turns her head
towards him and for a moment raises her paddle in salute.
On shore with his right arm raised, he is a solitary figure,
getting smaller and smaller, diminished
as we pull away and distance swells between us.
He looks so forlorn, I say, looking straight ahead
so that I don't see her reaction.
Yes is all she says.

ARCHIE BELANEY, NOTEBOOK, 1936

I really want her, but I'm not
going to do the coming.

She Loves You

You who know what's like to cut out a heart,
feel warm stickiness between your fingers,
sweet taste, succulent release,

I ask you: this fleshy emotion, this
tuber of memory, this deep, tell me where
inside, and I'll use my knife.

She loves you not

ARCHIE BELANEY, NOTEBOOK, 1936

Can't go on with this frustrated, dried out,
saintly,
unfulfilled, static, vegetating life.
My mind is empty, my soul shrivelling in a hard,
avaricious, narrow-minded (European) farmer's West.
Jealousy & meanness.

Beaver Lodge is truly a refuge
but is at times a cell! All night work,
never a day, eyes failing. No inspiration.
Speed was my god, 50 miles a day, 2,300 miles
one Summer, constant rapid travel. Now
nothing for the mind. I am supposed to keep on writing
about the bigger issues, broad, vast, deep (I speak often
in terms of Infinity), yet my life is circumscribed
confined as the beaver themselves.

I can see so far ahead. So much depends on me.
I am going to immortalize the Mississauga (River),
the Canadian north & the North American Indian.
I must keep going.

About a week from today I, along with thousands of other
interested sightseers, will witness one of the biggest Indian
conventions ever held in this part of the country, where bows and
arrows, peace pipes, long braided hair, buckskins, beads and feathers
and ancient ceremonial will play a very prominent role.

— *Grey Owl, Tales of an Empty Cabin, "Canadiana"*

JOHN TOOTOOSIS, 1936

We invite him into our circle to speak. We know who he is;
earlier we have seen him dance, or better I say try to dance.
He removes his hat and holds it with both hands as though
Wisahkecahk might snatch it from him and let it fly like a bird
in the grass. This man, who guided me around Ottawa, who
introduced me to the black suits in Indian Affairs,
who speaks face to face with the Prime Minister, is nervous
before our Council. Some of us smile in this knowledge
but no one lets out a sound. Each one who enters our circle
meets with respect.

In the prairie, in life, we are smaller than our words;
they are power. Our interpreter takes care, thinks through,
speaks loud and full so that everyone can hear and understand.
Wa-Sha-Quon-Asin, our Ojibway brother, tells us what he has
written in his books, what he has told the English, and what
he will tell Canada. I am only a poor half-breed, he says,
but like your man who swallows and reshapes my words,
I too am a two-voiced man. And I pledge to do whatever I can
for you. His words are straight and fly directly into the sun
and we cheer when he is finished. He wears himself with skill;
he has done a good service for his people.

We know Wa-Sha-Quon-Asin is not born of us, and we say nothing.
For us it is of no importance. We do not waste our words
but save them, because we know in this struggle of generations

they are our strongest medicine. This man flies for us true and
sharp, and we are thankful he has chosen our side. While
we cheer, and the elders nod in approval, we can see the light
shine in his face. We can see he feels better about himself
than before. This is good. This is how it should be,
to feel good about yourself and your duty in the honourable way.
Wa-Sha-Quon-Asin, we say, dance with us, as you can.

NO RETREAT

GREY OWL, 1936

There is no retreat. No rest. How can there be?
I'm invited to the Toronto Book Fair, and I pull myself
to it. From Beaver Lodge on Lake Ajawaan, I paddle 30 miles
to Waskesiu, the park headquarters, from where I travel
by truck, some 60 miles, into Prince Albert. There I board
a train and ride for 3 days. I cannot afford to pass up
the publicity (I keep reminding myself
every step of the way).

At the Crystal Ballroom where I'm scheduled to speak,
the organizers expect 800 people, 1,700 crowd into the room,
500 are turned away. Reporters pounce on me. I'm news,
and so I tell them Canada's heritage will be saved only
when Indians are made active partners in its preservation.

Some people in high places are worried. Very.
They say I'm becoming too political, others
like Governor General Lord Tweedsmuir
listen sympathetically
but do nothing.

ARCHIE BELANEY, NOTEBOOK, 1936

I am sick and scarcely able to walk
but don't expect to die for some time.

YVONNE PERRIER, 1936-37

How do you express yourself when you don't believe
such things really happen to people? Yvonne! Is this real?
Yvonne, wake up. We meet one evening in Ottawa
in the lounge of the Grads Hotel. Then he disappears
for nine months, and I get no more
than a couple of letters which don't say much
about his feelings, except
in regard to his beaver,
and the next time I see him,
he's talking marriage.

I'm with my girl friends. He's with a man friend.
They introduce themselves, and we're thrilled, absolutely.
We recognize him right away — I mean good heavens
his picture's in the paper — just as he recognizes
right away I'm Metis and moves to my side
of the table. Soon he's telling me about Jelly Roll
and Rawhide and Beaver Lodge and his tour of Britain,
which I find all so fascinating,
him being such a beautiful conversationalist.

He wants to know everything about me
and says although he must return to Prince Albert,
he'll write. For me it's hard to believe
a famous writer could possibly be interested in me,
a domestic, Dr. Elizabeth Shortt's helper.
He's my chance, my one chance,
and I'm not going to pass him by,
I say to myself without even knowing
if I'll ever hear from him again.

I mean how am I supposed to know if he's serious?
Sometimes when I'm cooking or cleaning
and my mind is a million miles away,
I find myself breaking into tears,
just thinking it would be better if I had never
set eyes on him. To put such hope into a person!
Why should I who have never had anything
suddenly expect to be swept away?

But one Saturday, there he is
at the door with a great big bouquet
of roses. I can hardly believe my eyes.
He's a handsome sight in a blue serge suit
with a black hat and a red silk scarf.
And talking so casually to Dr. Shortt, as if he knows her.
He asks to take me out to a restaurant,
and I look to the Doctor, who seems impressed
as me, and she tells me to go ahead
and enjoy myself.

And it's over dinner that he pops the question,
like he knows what he's doing, like the champagne
he's ordered. He jokes that at our age
we can't waste time. Well, he must be at least
a good ten years older than me,
but of course I agree.
There's no sense in either of us wasting time.
And that's it.
It's as simple as that.

TO: James A. Woods
       Superintendent, Prince Albert National Park,
       Saskatchewan

FM: Grey Owl

Keeping good as promised. Please
send 200. dollars
honeymoon expenses,
headoffice, Bank of Montreal.
            bonne fete
            Chief

GREY OWL, 1936

Honesty? You don't think I'm honest
   when I tell her I need her in my life,
   when I describe what it's like
   to live month after month alone in a cabin,
   where your only friends are animals.

Yes, I admit, I tell her my real name is McNeil
   and I was raised by an aunt, a school teacher,
   who lived near the Rio Grande.

Yes, I concoct this story to explain away my past
   so that I don't have to marry her as Belaney
   and risk getting charged with bigamy.

Dishonesty? Yes, I will even admit that. But
   let me ask you, Where is the harm? Compared
   to all those others who fill their pockets
   and become millionaires at the expense
   of the country, solely because of connections,
   because somehow they have access to Indian land,
   to timber, fur, booze, you name it.

Yes, compare me to those other so-called Great Canadians
   who pass and continue to pass their kind of legacy
   on to their heirs, always at the expense of the country.

Yvonne Perrier, 1936-37

We marry in Montreal, and he wraps me in furs
and takes me on an evening sleigh ride
up to Mount Royal where we watch the city lights
sparkle like candles on a giant snow cake,
which he says are nothing compared to the stars
of Lake Ajawaan.

The train ride to Prince Albert sees Archie plunge
into moods of silence or take out one of his bottles
and drink himself to sleep. Who is this stranger
I've married? How can we ever know who we've chosen?
I'm driven to ask as I watch him shivering
in the berth beside me, quietly moaning to himself.

We arrive on a fresh sun-drenched New Year's Day,
and he gives me a crash course in how to snowshoe
on our way to Beaver Lodge, while I teach him how to fall
on his back and make snow angels, and for awhile, lost
in one another's company, we laugh and play
and manage to forget we're adults.

In the cabin we dry off before a roaring fire, and
he confesses that he hasn't been this happy in years,
and it's when he says this that I see why I'm here.
As his wife, my job will be to keep him from himself,
to be his companion, his watchdog. For I also see
something inside him, something destructive,
like loneliness or pain, regret perhaps, something
he will never admit to.

The Thing About Photographs

hard to believe these photographs
actually drew breath
blew smoke rings
or kisses,
spoke in a voice that made you think spring break-up
or hot summer nights, cool fall, or even icy winter,
said come
or go
with lip and eye.

even he, whom the camera adores,
cannot believe it.
the thing is
everybody looks
the moment
as if that's all there is
or was
but there's more, he knows
only too well.

now that Gertie's gone
        his beloved Anahareo has made the break,
he too has to grab
and hold on.
Ajawaan is both sanctuary and prison,
nights so long,
he spends them counting stars,
wishing like a child,
like the man he is,
the gift of touch, breath, voice.

you see, the reel keeps turning
even after the camera has long stopped
and the pictures have been nicely framed
or neatly bound.
there is a click
and life goes on
in another direction.
the thing is
to get at that.

Yvonne Perrier, Silver Moon, 1937

You want to know how I got my name.
Have you ever been to northern Canada?
Correction.
Have you ever been to the untouched
north — in winter?

One January evening, after spending
the afternoon setting rabbit snares
on the edge of the park (I've told Archie
                    I know how to make a superb
                    rabbit stew)
we stop in the middle of the lake
for a breather, just to marvel
at the magic overhead.

Archie says he's been watching Ajawaan's sky
for nearly seven years now and it's always different
and yet the same — which is comforting.
The moon, I say, Nokomis, never looked so silver.
Yes, she remains always watchful and loving.
How many times did I stand out here, he says,
        raising his arms as though to embrace her,
        and then bringing them quickly to his chest,
Stand below her when I had no one else.
And now I have you, he turns to me,
and you are my Silver Moon.

GREY OWL, 1937

In August alone, a thousand visitors
make the trip to Beaver Lodge,
young and old alike, Americans,
Europeans, even a Viscount and a Major,
all while I'm busy preparing my lectures
for my second British tour.

They say a criminal always returns
to the scene of the crime. Certainly
this has nothing to do with me.
Still, what I want to know is
does he get away with it?

THE TALES

The sun burns itself
into remoteness.
Everything is changing,
has changed,
will change even more.
All there is left is sun
that is not sun, yet is sun.

What's left is to bury yourself
in past winters
to keep from freezing,
swing an invisible axe until you sweat.
To live yourself back
is to feel yourself
back in your own likeness.

JANE ESPANIEL, 1937

Come on Jane tell me, he insists. If you can't
then who can? We're just like brother and sister.
Honestly. The truth. I want to know
what you think of my tales.

Honestly? Sounds like a lot of north wind blowing.

MORT FELLMAN, 1937

The pieces fit together like the puzzle of a lifetime.
And not a single fact missing, I tell my City Editor.
Grey Owl's on his way to Abitibi country to make a film
and agrees to stop in North Bay to do an interview.
The train gets in at two o'clock so we agree to meet
at the Empire Hotel at three. I'm early,
but all the same he invites me to his room and greets me
warmly, while his wife takes my hat and coat
and then shows me to one of the two chairs by the window,
the one beside the dressing table, which I'm told I can use
to write on if I want. She even orders coffee.

You cannot meet Grey Owl and not be impressed. When
he speaks I listen in silence, in near abated breath,
half my mind focused on his words, the other half on the man
himself. The question that I so eagerly wanted to ask
soaring out of range. We, at the newspaper, have followed
this man, through his articles, through those written about him,
and even through people who say they know him personally.
Explain, I want to say. Explain.
And, yet, now that I'm here I hesitate and wait to hear
him out. Is it because I actually admire the man, his
commitment, what he stands for? I entered this room thinking
I've got him; this will be the story of the decade,
and now I find my tongue blunt as a hook cast
into the wind.

He goes on in a passionate but calm voice, a tirade against
what he calls the ignominious policies of the government
to let Canada fall into the maw of foreign companies,
giant amalgamations whose only concern is to get
what they can: if we don't watch out we won't even own
our birthright, poof and one day it'll be gone,
he says, looking out the window at the snow
making the sky look all feathery. This country
has the potential to be great, to be special,
built on respect for each other and our weaker brethren,
but it's being sold out, betrayed,

and for what, quick profit, more, more, more,
everybody wants more but will end up with nothing.

There is a woman in Temegami, a certain Angele Belaney,
who claims to be his wife — or at least one of them.
We checked it out and interviewed her,
and along with accounts from the locals the facts
seem to add up. According to her, she married an Englishman
named Belaney twenty-five years ago, whom she claims
is the same man who now calls himself Grey Owl,
or Archie NcNeil, or whatever his name is.

She lives in a shack with a daughter she also says is his,
and survives on rabbits, a far cry from how he's living,
thanks to his comfortable sinecure in the Park,
thanks to the dough he's raked in from his books
and recent tour of Britain. Yet, despite it all,
what seemed so clear-cut before entering this room
has become blurred like the iced-up weather:
it's as though there are two different and distinct
people, the Englishman who abandoned his Indian family
and this Indian man looking intently out the window.
Something no longer fits.

We cannot continue to see the wilderness simply as clutter
that must be got rid of, he now says. Look
what's happened to the great white pine
— all but extinct. Look what's happened to the soil,
the water, the animals,
and the men who had their place in that wilderness,
turned into vagrants
or labourers barely scraping a living.

While he pauses, I finish writing down what he's just said
and then look up to notice a bible on the night-table
beside the bed. He turns and notices me staring at it.
Do you read the bible? I ask,
curiously, though not naively.

Oh, that was here when we came, he says. I guess
in a place like this they figure there's always time
on one's hands for some inspirational guidance,
if you know what I mean.
And you? I ask.
As a boy I was forced to read it by a misguided aunt. But
faith can be had from many sources, from Nature for example,
from watching sunlight play upon autumn leaves.
Speaking of your aunt, I interrupt — seeing my chance —
it's now or never. Would you happen to know
anyone by the name of Belaney?

The conversation comes to an immediate halt.
He doesn't answer but instead turns towards his wife
and asks her for the time.
She tells him and he says that she should show me out.
One more question, I break in and ask.
There will be no more questions, he answers, in a curt voice
that is the sound of an axe splitting a frozen block of wood.
And I keep quiet, not daring to stick out my neck
any further than it already is.

What more is there to know? I ask
Mr. Bunyan, the City Editor, back at the office.
Grey Owl, McNeil, Belaney they're one and the same.
But according to him, the question now becomes
what good will it do to expose him? For a newspaperman
nothing should be taken in isolation, he says,
everything must be weighed
against some other element in the story: you know,
don't get lost in the trees looking for the forest.
Obviously, it wouldn't do any good.
So what do we do?
Wait, he says.

Wait? For what?

It's simply not the right time, he answers
matter-of-factly, as he folds the paper he's been reading
and tosses it into the wastepaper basket. Today's news,
tomorrow's trash, he smiles. Don't
get your britches in a twist,
I'll tell you when it's time
to put together your story.
And that's how it ends. Just like that.
Mr. Grey Owl,
McNeil,
Belaney is off the hook. For now.

ARCHIE BELANEY, NOTEBOOK, 1937

People think I am masquerading,
think that the beaver is my living.
They do not understand.

ANGELE LOVES HER ENGLISHMAN

Even after she heard all the stories about Archie,
his drinking and fighting, about other wives
and children, heard that what he had told her
about his birth in Mexico, his Apache mother,
had been childhood fantasy, even after she heard
that as Grey Owl he had made all kinds of money,
which neither she nor their daughter ever saw,
even after all that, she still loved him,
considered him a good man,
her man.

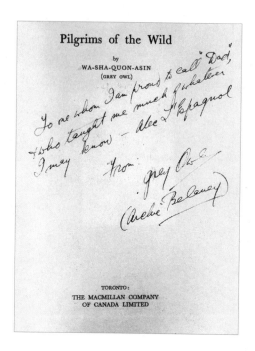

Pilgrims of the Wild
by
WA-SHA-QUON-ASIN
(GREY OWL)

To me whom I am proud to call "Dad,"
(who taught me much of whatever
I may know) — Alec L'Espagnol
from: grey Owl.
(Archie Belaney)

TORONTO:
THE MACMILLAN COMPANY
OF CANADA LIMITED

ANNIE ESPANIEL, 1937

He's come to Bisco to make a movie about the Mississauga River,
going to make what he calls his dream picture. Almost everybody
in town goes out to the station to meet him. It's like a party
with Archie the centre of attraction. After greeting old friends and
acquaintances he sees me and comes over to where I'm standing
back aways from the crowd and introduces his new wife, Yvonne.
Then he says, Shall we go home? Just like that. On our way,
he asks where's Dad, my husband Alex, supposing he's busy
in the bush guiding tourists. He doesn't seem to notice my look,
and at first I don't answer. Finally I tell him. He died.

Archie's sitting at the kitchen table with his hands clasped
to a cup of tea. It's late. His wife has gone to bed. Archie
never did sleep much, and besides he's still in shock to hear
it happened just last August. He finds it hard to believe
it could happen so suddenly and to such a strong and active man
like my husband: trapper, hunter, guide, tourist operator,
prospector, kind and gentle man — nobody ever went away hungry

from our door. I tell him not to be foolish, we can never know
when it's our time, and he should take better care of himself.

How? He wants to know.
Something inside him, I answer.
Did he see a doctor?
He was too sick to travel.
Couldn't one have come from Chapleau or Sudbury?
You know no doctor will come for Indian people, I say and see
him lose his white face to a red one. Mad, he bangs his hand
down on the table and spills his tea, and quickly apologizes
but looks on helplessly without making a move.

It's me who jumps up to wipe the mess, while Archie continues
to talk and just wait for me to finish. He wants to know if Alex
received the book he sent. The one with the inscription in it:
To One Whom I Am Proud to Call Dad.
Yes, I say, at the sink ringing out the cloth. He got the book.
Archie smiles knowing this.
Hope he liked it? he asks, unsure, hinting.

He did, I answer. He was happy to see how much you learned.
And for a while we're quiet, both lost to the old days.

Like the time when I was cleaning and found the blasting caps
underneath Archie's bed — and was going to kick him out
when my husband said he'd talk to the boy and teach him
the Indian way. Imagine, Grey Owl blowing up beaver houses.
Or the times Archie kept us up night after night
with his out-of-tune singing and drumming until I asked Alex
to please make him stop or at least get someone to show him how.

Or when Archie insisted that we speak Indian to him because
he wanted to learn the language. Come first light
Alex would be yawning and Archie would still be asking him
questions. A good listener, a regular still-hunter,
Alex would tell me the next day. And if that wasn't enough,

like the time I searched high and low for my Indian prayer book
only to discover Archie had it. He was reading it
to get the words right.

Like those times, and our Christmases together, when
they came out of the bush with enough fur to buy clothes
and sweets for all the kids, and what a feast we'd have,
everyone together, laughter and music.
Archie. Do you remember Christmas together? I ask,
leaving my dream and returning to the room
to see him wiping his eyes.

ARCHIE BELANEY, NOTEBOOK, 1937

Early days everything rip tearing speed.
After meeting Alex Espaniel more calm and quiet,
contentment, little intimate enjoyments,
appreciating bush in its finest sense.

MISSISSAUGA BACK

Mississauga is mood. Feel it.
See. Re-
Member.
Be.

Make the trip,
and your strip of film
is a birchbark canoe shooting water
that leaps and boils white
compressed and spun hard by walls of granite.
Holler and paddle, paddle for all you're worth,
for the dream of a lifetime of being here,
the adrenaline fire, the charge, the fury,
and the laughter that follows over a good drink of bushtea.

Slide now and relax into deep black calm, past islands
where pine, birch and poplar stand untouched
and like an old brigade cast shadows of friendship,
where trout jump circles of time
more solid and silver
than all the money in the world.

Mississauga, fresh and potent
as birth, ultimate and final
as death, first and last experience,
beginning and end
of North America,
mystery and faith.
Back we go, camera
in mind.

ARCHIE GREY OWL, 1937

I let Antoine take the stern of the canoe.
You sure? he says. It's your picture.
That's exactly why I want you there, I tell him.
I can see he's glad I've given the steering over
to him. Something he would never say. In front of us
is the gauntlet, a roaring cataclysmic mile of white water,
which my cameraman is to film us swooping down. Even in
the calmer parts of these waters I'm finding difficulty
keeping the canoe under control, let alone
guide us down these thunder-drum rapids.

No, it's better this way. To put it plainly,
my strength's gone. What I took for granted
ten years ago I can't imagine myself doing today.
To think about it hurts. Hurts bad. Too long
pushing paper, that's what's wrong with me.
My last run, the least I can do is go out with style
and finesse, without having the world see me tumble
head and tea kettle into my immortal Mississauga,
some posthumous glory that would be.

Little out of practice, I yell over the noisy water.
Anyway, it's time we ancients gave you younger men a chance
to see what you can do. Antoine just gives me a quick
concentrated grin. He's one of the best. We both know
this way there'll be no unexpected problems.
He makes no comment, except to ask me where exactly
I would like the canoe to come down
for the perfect camera angle,
and I thank him for this,
Ojibway brother.

Ellen Elliott, 1937

After shooting his winter film in Abitibi, Grey Owl
comes to Toronto where he and Bert Bach, his cameraman,
work on the edit at the Macmillan office. To say the time
we spend with him is a trial of endurance is to be kind
and to put it mildly. Now let me see, something nice to say
about the man? I could say he comes across looking good
on film. He's a marvelous snow-shoer.
He treats his dog team well, better in fact
than he treats his wife
who ends up sitting in the hotel room with him
— when he's persuaded to take a break —
watching him pour gallons of beer down his gullet.
His idea of a good time.

Too much for all concerned, far too much, it turns out
that he has to be taken care of twenty-four hours a day.
Yvonne can't leave him alone for five minutes
or else he heads straight for the bar,
or disappears only goodness knows where.
Her coaxing him to stop, or at least slow down
doesn't do any good, so finally I step in and threaten
to cut our funding for the project
if he comes into the office once more,
8:00 in the morning! mind you,
with alcohol on his breath.

One thing I will say for him though,
despite it all, he's a devil for work. We all see
the rough shape he's in and can't help but wonder
what keeps him going. Is it the drink?
Bert says up north Grey Owl's coughing was so bad
that on a couple of occasions they thought he was choking
to death. They got scared and suggested postponing
the shoot, but he wouldn't hear of it.

The truth is to watch him on film is to see how gaunt
and worn-out he is, slipping almost staggering
down a bank of snow, straining

under a weight his companions carry effortlessly,
even Yvonne doing a much better job of it
than the old pro himself.
Get him to bed, I say to her.
She says she's tried,
but it's useless to talk to him.
He's got his own mind, and his own way,
and he won't let anyone near him —
let alone inside him — to interfere in the least.

Two unforgettable weeks too long,
and with his wife in tow, Grey Owl heads back
to Lake Ajawaan, where he's going to work
on the film's captions as well as another book,
before setting off on another tour
of Britain. How much more?
How much more can he take?
Can anyone?

SNOWSHOES

He remembers barely able to walk,
fitting on his first snowshoes
and falling,
falling into windswept snow,
struggling to stand.
Knowing this failure as his own
whiteness, he dreamed
always dreamed of the day
he would learn

(it all, to split ash, heat it over a fire
to make it workable, to weave
a spidery pattern of sinew and raw moosehide).

And the day came, no, it was night.
He doesn't remember exactly
when, because
it came gradually like the wearing
down of the season.
He stood, walked, and then even ran.
Twirled round and called out
to Basshkaakodin Giizis,
the freezing moon,
come dance.

Grey Owl, Grey Owl

Where
Have you been?
I've been to London
To visit the King
And the Queen.
Grey Owl,
Grey Owl.
What did you do there?
I spoke of my people.
My philosophy
I wanted to share.
Grey Owl,
Grey Owl. What did you say?
That we need their help.
Rejected, dejected,
We live in dismay.
Grey Owl,
Grey Owl. How
did they react?
They smiled with sympathy,
And said, Is that a fact.
Grey Owl, Grey Owl
Did they agree?
It's difficult to tell.
We'll just have to wait
And see.

Yvonne Perrier-O'Neil (Belaney), Silver Moon

Here I am wearing a silk gown,
the latest fashion,
something I would never have dared dream of owning.
We are on our way to Buckingham Palace
where Grey Owl, my husband,
will give a Command Performance
for the Royal family.

When he proposed, he said, Yvonne,
for better or for worse,
no matter what happens,
marry me and you will go places,
see something other than the same Ottawa streets,
the same dirty floors and dishes.
Yes, I said, and held my breath.
And here I am, like magic.

I can feel there's a lot he hasn't told me.
That I'm exhausted from taking care of him,
(no small feat, believe me).
But right now I'm riding in a shiny carriage
with my buckskin Prince,
on my way to once in a lifetime,
and I couldn't care less.

LOVAT DICKSON, 1937

By this time you've read it in the newspapers. All I will add
is that by now Grey Owl is more a dramatic raconteur
than a writer, performing like a professional, as smooth
as the gold silk that adorns the Throne Room. This is not
to say I'm calm, far from it; the very idea of him lecturing
at Buckingham Palace makes me jump back to the times
he's needed supervision, if not to be reprimanded.
My mind back there, I see him exploding like a moonshiner's still
and telling some profane bushwhacker joke, and the Queen
holding the ears of Princess Elizabeth or little Margaret Rose,
while the King points a finger and orders his footmen
to escort him out, at once. Then again, deep down
in that same river of running thought, there is a voice
telling me he can handle it like child's play,
like the children he will undoubtedly play up to.

With Grey Owl you never know when there will be cause
for hair-pulling pandemonium. And there certainly is
a flush of panic when he decides to shred protocol and
announces that the King and Royal family are to be seated
before he, Grey Owl, Emissary of Canada's Indian people,
makes his appearance. He will have it no other way
and threatens to call the whole thing off:
temperamental obstinacy, a case of nerves, second thoughts,
for lack of a better explanation. But the hissed hysteria
of palace officials soon makes way to last minute diplomacy,
and the King gives his consent and is seated, when the great
oak doors are flung open and Grey Owl, like both a mythic
and modern Hiawatha rolled into one, enters and majestically
raises his arm in peace and friendship, and thus the show begins
to the pleasure of all concerned.

(I say show because that's what I feel it really is, theatre,
and although we're making a fortune, 3,000 people in one seating,
I'm looking forward to the end of it all in a fortnight. After
3 months, 33 cities, 138 lectures, 4,350 miles, this half-breed,
whom I first brought to Britain two years ago from the wilds of
northern Canada, when he was an unknown author with a vague

plan to save the beaver, and who has since attained what few men
ever dream of, who has so enthralled and frustrated me, sails away
for America to return never more.)

We arrive at the palace at 3:00 sharp, and stay for three hours,
much longer than planned. After the lecture the Royal family speaks
with Grey Owl and Silver Moon for another half hour.
Grey Owl uses this time to describe for the King the plight
of Canada's Indian people. Speaks of old-time independence
and dignity that has been stripped from them. Tells
how their traditional homelands have been decimated,
clear-cut, mined and flooded. Explains that they
have become squatters in their own land, because of what
he calls civilized greed. Says they must be allowed
back to the forests before it's too late
and there are no forests left, before everything is polluted
and dead. Implores that it is they, not white people,
who should be put in charge of Canada's forests and wildlife.
The King appears interested, listens attentively and asks
questions. At the end of their conversation, Grey Owl
shakes his hand, proud of himself, pleased with what
he has managed to do today.

Outside, in the wet air, on this December 10,
illness forgotten,
Grey Owl is again a young man.

Cities. Towns. Audiences. Halls. Stages.
One after another
after one. After.
How do you keep going? When all
is given & all is all there is.
When your eyelids say NIBAAN.
Sleep, but you can't & say No, KAWEEN.
When they say NIBAADAA.
Together let us sleep.
And you say No, KAWEEN.
When they say NIWINIBAA.
I am going to sleep.
And you repeat No, KAWEEN.

Forever & Ever. Dream Catcher. You.

How to keep going when damp has soaked your bones
wobbly. When unheated halls whistle
& the audiences clamour for more
as though you were fat
when really you are thin
as the paper the room wants to blow away.
Weak. So.
Many. Always another week.
Another morning, evening, into car, into train,
into body,
out of mind.
into time & storm,
                    itinerary
                         storm: Oct. 25th London...
                                   Oct. 26th Manchester...
                                   Oct. 27th Liverpool...
Oct. 28th Bournville... Oct. 29th Leeds... Oct. 30th Birmingham...
Oct. 31st Brighton... Nov. 1st it's Crowborough... Nov. 2nd Bath...
Nov. 3rd Exeter... Nov. 4th Torquay... Nov. 5th Bournemouth...
Nov. 6th Howe... Nov. 8th Bristol... Nov.9th Cheltenham... Nov.
11th Salisbury... Nov. 12th Sheffield... Nov. 13th York... Nov.14 &
15th Newcastle... Nov. 16 Whitley Bay... Nov.17th Windermere...

Nov. 18th Perth... Nov. 19th Dundee & St. Andrews... Nov.20th Helensburgh... Nov. 22nd Paisley... Nov.23rd & 24th Glasgow... Nov. 26th & 27th Edinburgh... Nov. 29th Bexhill... Nov. 30th Oxford... Dec. 1st Southport... Dec. 2nd Liverpool... Dec. 3rd Sunderland... Middlesboro... Darlington... Scarborough... Harrogate... Bradford... Lincoln... Buckingham Palace... Tunbridge Wells... Hastings... Ipswich... Cambridge... Norwich... London...

Weak.

MATTHEW HALTON, 1937

Coming from Alberta, Pincher Creek to be exact, born
and raised almost next door to the Peigan Indian Reserve,
it's not as if I've never seen or spoken to an Indian before.

Here in London people are coming out in droves to hear
the famous Grey Owl. As a correspondent for the Toronto Star
I ask myself how can I possibly get an interview. The problem
is how to arrange it, especially as he's already swamped
with reporters and has a schedule of lectures and appointments
jam-packed. I get the idea to leave him a message and
sign it from a fellow Canadian. Sure enough he agrees
to meet me. It turns out the only time he has available
is while having his portrait done.

I arrive at the artist's studio the next day, a murky afternoon,
and sit across from where Grey Owl's posing. Stark light
from the skylight filters over him, making his gaunt
grayish features appear more ghostly than real. I'm entranced,
soaking in all that he says. He's unlike anyone I've ever met.
His message is new, unlike anything I've ever heard before,
him boldly telling me that mankind is a stampeding herd
lost to the machine — and I'm reminded that over the wires
reports of the fascists are beginning to come in daily.

We speak for over an hour, during which time he sits motionless,
refusing to take a break, wanting to get it over with.
On the surface there appears nothing complex about him: modest
and reserved, a man outside looking in, a man living far away
from civilization who has come for a short visit (a point
he makes sure to emphasize), a man as natural and unsullied
as the great northern lakes, out of place in a modern world
where progress means dams and automobiles and smokestacks.

I cannot help but admire him, believe in his integrity,
the ideal to which he aspires. Yet, at the same time,
I get the impression there is something below the surface
— the sketch of charcoal, the pigment on canvas —
which is as turbulent as any machine or London street.

Before parting we shakes hands and he thanks me for helping
him pass on his message. We are outside and he's late
for another appointment. I turn back to wave, but
he's already given himself up to a furnace of pedestrians,
rushing like a clock about to explode. Later
I unwittingly report in my article,
the problem with Grey Owl
is that he appears too good to be true.

WHAT DOES IT TELL YOU?

After lecturing non-stop for a month
he finally decides to take a one day holiday
and uses it to drive to a zoo near Birmingham, 400 miles,
to check on a beaver he's heard is living in misery.

Witnessing a cement cage, he tracks down the superintendent
and (shall I say) firmly suggests — using his fame
for leverage to move the man off his fat rump —
certain necessary changes like water and trees.

A month later when the lecture tour takes him to Birmingham,
he makes sure
at the first opportunity
to return to the zoo (and is much relieved).

ARCHIE BELANEY, NOTEBOOK 1937

My heart
is in it
with both feet.

GREY OWL, 1937

Hastings must be included. I don't care what city
has to be cut from the itinerary, but Hastings
is the one place I want on the tour.
I get a puzzled look. I know we're booked solid as ice,
sold out, tied up, and running on empty,
but I'm adamant. I've got friends there,
who helped me convalesce during the war,
who took care of me,
were kind to me. And we of the old school
never forget our friends. Sure enough,
my publisher, the head honcho of this whirlwind extravaganza,
finds a free afternoon
and squeezes in my request.

December 14, driving out from London, I am on my way back
to the land of what I thought was no return,
and I find myself eager as one of my... (no I won't say it)
even though I know someone in the audience
might easily pick me off, accuse me
of being nothing more than an old school mate.
Archie is that you? I can hear them now.
Yet, there's no need for alarm. Did I not paddle effortlessly
through this same route a couple of years ago
on my last tour without running aground?
Did they not rush up to me for my autograph
like everywhere else? So why should this time
be any different?

And even if there were a problem brewing,
I would risk it all for the chance to see my Aunt Ada
and Carrie's reaction
when I tell them that a week ago their Archie
gave a Command Performance at Buckingham Palace,
and not only saw the Royal family
but actually spoke to them and shook the hand

of the King, himself. Called him Brother.
What do you think of that!
I'll say. Can't go any higher.
And I know they will be pleased pink, if not astounded
and speechless, to know
that I haven't merely made something of myself,
but have risen far beyond what they ever thought
of me, beyond their piddling imaginations
to the very height of kings.

GREY OWL, 1937

M-o-t-h-e-r! I wanted so many times to scream.
And, now, after I had thought I would never need you,
made a point of not needing you, or seeing you,
I come to you, weary thin, to postpone the inevitable
what must be, my crust moon break-up, my decline,
as the old foretell, my circle complete.

For you dear Mother, whom I've resented all these years
for leaving me behind, the day you remarried
and forgot all about me, who bore a child
named Archibald Stansfeld Belaney, know who I am,
and can shatter me like the looking-glass
I once bought you for a birthday present.
Do you remember it Mother? how you held it
in your slender hand and combed your long dark hair.
How I loved to sit quietly and watch you. And how one day
with those same hands you held me and said you had to go,
and from now on I was to live with my aunties.
No, I wanted to be with you.
Please don't go, I cried.

Then I got mad and said you were just like him,
father, the man I had never seen, and you slapped me
and I grabbed that beautiful looking-glass,
which I had bought especially for you
with the pennies I had saved, where
I had seen your face shine on so many evenings,
and I threw it on the floor and it cracked
and fell to pieces just as your beauty and love
fell to pieces that day when you packed your bags
and walked out the door, my tears
making you forever ugly. Even when you came to visit
I no longer saw the person you once were,
but what you had become, a stranger
with a cold face and a colder heart, nothing
could ever again be the same. I too would leave,
leave and never return.

KITTIE (BELANEY) SCOTT-BROWN, 1937

I hear he's lecturing in Oxford, and having no alternative I go
to his hotel. I need to see him desperately.
At this point I have no idea that he also needs to see me.
Although I bore him, I never raised him, and this
he has always held against me. How does one explain?
after so many years — tell the truth,
that circumstances were beyond my control and
did not permit it. I am nervous, too many years have passed,
far too many to even call him my son. And, yet,
when your own flesh and blood attains such heights,
how can you not feel something, be thankful and proud.
I decide to wear my best black dress,
a bit faded, but still serviceable and I think proper
for the occasion.

He is between lectures when I call and have a note
of introduction brought to his room. The response is prompt
and positive. I am to meet him upstairs. A bellboy escorts me
up, and Grey Owl, my Archie, if I can call him that,
greets me at the door with a formal handshake
and leads me to a large sitting room, where he introduces me
as an old friend to his attractive wife Silver Moon.
We have barely time to exchange pleasantries,
before Archie quickly interrupts
and asks her if she wouldn't mind seeing about some tea.
She takes the hint. And actually,
I find myself quite relieved
because what I want to ask him is difficult enough
without company.

He's courteous but cold and distant, doing his utmost
to keep a rather grim expression on his face.
It's when I mention his childhood in Hastings
that I see him get truly upset. Clearly,
I will have to explain my side of his story.
To begin, I tell him I was young,
too young and too dependent,
and another marriage was the only way out for me. Try

to understand, I say. I was abandoned. I had no choice.
I could no longer live in that house
and be treated like a piece of cast-off clothing.
He is quiet for a moment,
and I don't know what to expect — I am preparing myself
to stand and leave, when he touches my hand
and looks me straight in the face
with his blue eyes, the baby eyes I remember,
and says quietly that he understands.

Before I leave, I ask him for what I've come for.
Money to help support his brother Hugh,
who has never recovered from the war.
Because of his mental illness the expenses
incurred are far more than I can afford. I need help.
There is only one condition, he says: from this moment on
you have never met Grey Owl in your life,
nor will you ever mention his name
to a living soul. Yes, you are a man with a soul,
I tell him. It's not easy for a mother to give up a son.
Nor is it any easier to see another suffer.
Take care of Hugh, are his last words,
along with good-bye.

KEN CONIBEAR, 1937

I'm beside him every day. Eat with him. Drive with him.
Talk with him. We even drink together. On occasion,
although booze I try to keep away from him. Call him renowned
author and conservationist, driven alcoholic and best man
at my wedding. Call me companion, manager, chauffeur,
trouble-shooter, watch-dog. After writing one and a half novels
I'm stuck and broke and literally on the verge of starvation
when Mr. Dickson of Lovat Dickson Ltd. of London,
formerly of Alberta and an English instructor, hires me
to accompany Grey Owl across Britain on his tour.
My credentials, Rhodes Scholar raised as far north
as you would ever want to go, Fort Resolution
and Fort Smith, Northwest Territories. Ask me about Indians,
grew up with them, Chipewyan, Dogrib. Sure I'll do it, I say.
Would be honoured.

130 lectures, 4,300 miles (so far), and he's not missed or been late
for one. This morning the sky is again grey overcast,
the road wet and muddy. Rows of trees, drenched and slumped,
appear in the mist like a ragged column of soldiers.
Grey Owl is riding up front with me and, I notice,
he's in an especially relaxed mood, his usual pensive
silence has made way to casual banter; at the moment
he's referring to the soggy countryside and
how at least they don't have to worry about forest fires.
Yvonne is napping in the back seat. After spending
an enjoyable evening in Oxford, we're once again speeding
towards our next stop, this time Southport,
where judging from advanced ticket sales
the hall will be teeming with anxious spectators.

He asks me at what time we're expected to arrive
and my eyes are off the road for no more than a second
when it happens, a tire blows and the car suddenly careens
and skids to the right. I hear Yvonne wake and cry out
at the same time as I turn the wheel hard left and
step on the brake, but the car doesn't respond
and Grey Owl yells hold on and the first thing I know

we're off the road and through a hedge
and abruptly stopped. Fortunately we've survived unscathed,
merely shaken up a bit, and the Vauxhall is no worse
for wear and tear. Expecting him to be upset with me
for not watching the road, I'm waiting for the crunch
when all he does is pat me on the shoulder and say,
Boy! that sure was a change of pace, great fun!
We change the tire and with Yvonne in the driver's seat
manage to push it back onto the road. When we finally arrive
at Cambridge Hall a thousand people have been waiting
for over an hour.

The local organizer explains what has happened, and
the moment Grey Owl climbs on to the podium the room breaks
into a standing ovation. Once again he has them in the palm
of his hand, which makes me think of the little white pills
he's been pouring into his hands and popping into himself.
Pills to pick him up or calm him down, I don't know
which and neither does his wife. Although listening to him
up there speaking from his heart, a heart that's now cut wide
open and beating for all to see and hear, his notes
long ago abandoned, I am once again mesmerized and recognize
that the only thing that really matters is what he has to say.
Each night I find myself sitting in the wings listening to him
again and again, ignoring the work I'm supposed to be doing —
such as organizing the book stand — enthralled as much as ever,
as though this was the first time I'd ever heard him,
as though I'd never laid eyes on him before.

During our drive towards London I ask him frankly. How is it
each lecture is so unique, so different from the previous one?
At first he doesn't answer, and then he says, How is it birds
find their way home each year? Because it's in them
just as what I do is in me. I open myself and out fly my words.
In this way each audience gets a lecture tailor-made for them.
He's pleased with his answer and doesn't elaborate further
because it seems to me this is what he believes. I too
am satisfied. A fine man, doing something for his people,

I'm thinking, when suddenly a lorry pulls up beside us
at a stop and two young men begin to yell at him and
make child-like whooping sounds with their hands
slapping their lips. Before I can even say ignore them,
Grey Owl is out of the car brandishing his hunting knife,
and the two men are out of the cab and running down the road.
I catch up to him and tell him it's OK, there's no harm done,
let them go.

I need a beer he says when we're back on the road,
and I can see that he means it. Yvonne speaks up and says
perhaps we can get something before the next talk.
It won't be the first time he's gone on stage with a few drinks
under his belt. A couple of times last week he was downright
drunk, but always he managed to sober up on the podium
and, most amazingly, to the delight of the audience,
come flying to a grand finale. By the time the autographing
session began his true condition was imperceptible to all
but us, who had to supply him with large glasses of milk
to settle his stomach and douse the fire inside him.
There is silence now in the car, as though we are waiting
for something else to erupt, for eventual rain perhaps.
Nothing. The sky remains heavy, and with our destination
in sight, he apologizes for the stir he was caught in
back there, and everything once again is back to normal.
Caught, that's what I hear him say. Caught in the wheels
of a mad civilized world and speeding beyond control,
a bush Indian out of the bush, is what I'm thinking.

ARCHIE BELANEY, NOTEBOOK, 1937

The whole landscape seems to engulf me
so that I am a part of it and it of me.
I am no longer in
            but of the forest.

NIGHT

WA-SHA-QUON-ASIN

By midnight
the house sleeps
while I'm in bed with
eyes open. Embers
stirred in darkness

I AM

After three lectures
and hours
of signing books,

HE

too exhausted

WHO WALKS BY NIGHT

to even think
of arguing
with my fountain pen,

I SAY

I dress to go out
into the foggy street
or
down into the parlour
to play the gramophone
and drink scotch.

HE IS ME

Tonight
without hope in sight
of losing this
insomnia
I've become

WA-SHA-QUON-ASIN

LOVAT DICKSON, 1937

Yesterday the BBC refused to allow Grey Owl to broadcast
his farewell speech to the children of Britain
because his script mentions fox hunting, a controversy
they prefer to avoid.

It can only be discussed in a debate which argues both the pros and
the cons, the official said, ensconced behind a large desk.

What are you talking about? he replied. What pros?
A defenseless fox is torn to pieces
by men and women with a horde of dogs,
and you have the gall to call that sport? Tradition?

Today he's shouldering this failure as though the whole tour
depended on that one broadcast. They pushed a brick wall
down on him, and he's going away a broken man,
humbled by defeat.
Close, he says. I was so close, and he holds his thumb and forefinger
a fraction of an inch apart.
Forget it, I respond. Look what you've accomplished.
I try to convince him before he boards the SS Berengaria.

How will he do it? Tour the United States and Canada
for another three months. With those vast distances,
he'll have to spend all his time traveling, hours
and hours, jostled from one train to the next.
And in his condition. In the frozen heat
of sub-zero temperatures. Impossible.
Go back home to Beaver Lodge and rest, I almost say,
but don't because I know it would do no good.
Just as I know this sadness that now threatens
to overwhelm me is for a friend in need,
a friend I will never see again.

Back and forth across the American - Canadian border, broken
by this perpetual deluge like a branch off a tree. Adrift.

	Ottawa		New York
Toronto	Quebec City		Montreal
Pittsburgh	Springfield		Boston
Peterborough	Milwaukee		Hamilton
Providence	Kenosha		Port Hope
Buffalo		Detroit	London
Regina...Toronto		Windsor	

No pool of calm. No rest. No power but will. I go on.

JACK LEVE, 1938

I happen to be in New York meeting with some fur buyers
when I read that Archie's also in the city.
He's happy to hear from an old Bisco friend and invites me
over to his room. Says he's got something he wants to show me.

If it isn't Trader Jack, after all these years, he greets me,
as soon as I step into the room, which turns out to be smaller
than I expected for such a famous fellow like him.
Thought they would have put you in the Presidential Suite,
I joke, and he shrugs, unconcerned or resigned,
as he goes over to the night-table and picks up a bottle
of Johnny Dewar's Extra Special and tosses it to me.
Pour yourself your own poison, he says.
Archie's been drinking, and I know what that means.
So with glass in hand, I sit down
while he goes over and opens a movie projector screen.

Then he begins to explain what he's doing here in New York.
It's my mission, he says, but ask me
if I feel like I'm beating my head against a brick wall.
People come to see the cigar store Indian, the spectacle,
not to hear my message. What they want is entertainment,
value for their dollar. For all they care,
the Indian can go the way of the buffalo,
and they'll even help us along — which isn't to say
they haven't. It's all the same to them, the past,
maybe dress it up and bring it out once a year for a rodeo
or a circus. What counts is profit, how much money
can be made off it. You should know Jack with your years
of buying and selling. Take a look around. Look
at this city. Have you ever seen anything so primitive
in your life?

Archie! I interrupt,
before he goes on, before I correct myself,
Grey Owl, I mean.
I don't want to alarm him, but I'm aghast to see him
in this condition, this once rough-tough wilderness man

sitting here half-stewed with his face puffed up
like a bullfrog, his body like a willow in the wind.
Old before his time.
Excuse me for asking, but are you feeling all right?
Well enough to keep going, he answers. Another couple of months
and it'll be all over anyway, and I'll be heading north.
To my beaver and peace and quiet. Away from this hysteria.
He doesn't want to be here, but he's of the old school and
this is what he's committed to, bound himself
to follow to the bitter end. And so I ask,
What is it you wanted me to see?

The Mississauga, he says aloud, his voice changing tone
and taking on an air of excitement I can feel
just by sitting next to him. The Mississauga
right here in the room. I've already watched it twice today,
and nearly every day. This is what keeps me going Jack.
When I have no more energy, I look to this film for inspiration,
for trees and hills and valleys and, not least, white water,
which to me in it's pure magnificence comes closer to God
than anything man can ever hope to emulate.
And I say to myself, this is why I'm here,
this is what it's all about.
And with the flick of the light, the projector starts
and Grey Owl's right, the Mississauga is inside the room.
Silent on the screen, yet, loud, because
we've both been there and know
the unspeakable moods of it, and down deep, down
a crystal voice fills our ears, as we sit and drink
our drinks in awed wonder.

I show them the film, and I try to get it through their heads
that the wilderness is worth saving, he later says.
I don't know, sometimes I think it's sinking in,
other times aaahhh. What's the use?
I feel like packing up and leaving,
stick to writing books and not have to face anyone.
One thing I do know, this is it for me, he adds after a pause,

with the finality of his clenched fist. No more.
Of course I believe him, and so I mention the article about him
in Time magazine. They say he's had seven wives.
He says he knows about it. And I nod and wait for him
to explain, add something, anything, which he doesn't,
and I think what else is there he's not telling?
Grey Owl, I finally say, remember back when you were just Archie,
and we went to Montreal together. I had some business there,
must've been back around 1924, and we went to that Cowboy
and Indian movie, and you stood up halfway through
and started yelling
they had no right to kill your brothers.

Do you remember?
He remembers, he says, smiling devilishly.
Well, that was quite the show you put on, wasn't it?
Until the ushers came and threw you out. Careful, I say,
be careful, as I hoist myself out of the chair to greet
his new wife who has just walked into the room.

GREY OWL, 1938

Where are the buffalo? Gone the way of the Indian.

In the United States I lecture to professors and lawyers
and bankers and dentists,
people who want to see and be seen
with the famous writer,
naturalist
and hopeless dreamer,
the one and only Grey Owl.

Professionals who have no more interest in what I say
than Hitler or Mussolini, whom the newspapers show ranting
and raving nearly every day.

Conservation? What's that? Something to drink?
We can't even stop killing ourselves,
how can we possibly stop
killing Nature?

Where is the Indian? Gone the way of the buffalo.

GREY OWL, 1938

5th Avenue, people rushing from buildings and noise rushing
from traffic, much too much, locked and trying to break free,
to continue on my way, but held fast.

Faker, the man taunts. Faker, he says again, and I try
to ignore him and his venomous mouth, his peeled-back eyes,
while pedestrians stop to watch the commotion,
gather and shove,
and before I know it I'm breathing in his steam.

Come clean, he spits, and I try to push him away.
But where? The crowd surges and he pushes back, and I find
myself tethered between bodies. And that's when I react
and reach for my trusty knife and hear Yvonne say No,
the same moment my American agent, Colston, gasps
and grabs my arm to pull me away. Another time, another place,
he wouldn't have been able to stop me so easily.

I'm surprised by my own weakness and, like Colston, I curse
under my breath, but not the troublemaker we've left behind,
rather myself for being stuck here in this no man's land,
useless, worn-out, dead on my feet. Which makes me mad as hell
because I can't die, not here, not yet.

Afterwards Colston paces the room, rubs his hands nervously,
wipes his brow with his hanky. You can't do that, he says.
You just can't make a scene like that. Maybe in England
but not here in America. You've got to remember, on this side
of the Atlantic there are people — law biding, upstanding
citizens — who still believe the only good Indian is a dead one.
I'm not saying everybody, but there are some for sure. They hear
your "Tree" story about paleface soldiers and ruthless suppression
of the American Indian, certainly they get riled. You're bound
to get a few hotheads after you.

As for the press, sure they're on your side right now, but
don't kid yourself, that could change overnight. You know what
they'll do if they get a taste of something they don't like.
Spit you out. That's what. You could say goodbye
to your lecture tour, if not your career as a writer.
They'd either paint you to look like a sullen, dangerous,
savage who should be locked up or a fork-tongued charlatan
with something to hide, and who doesn't have something to hide?

It's your choice, Chief. But remember, right now you're an idol,
and with the kind of money you're making you can afford
to turn the other cheek.

TAP

You sit in your darkened hotel room next to the window. You
have been sitting the whole night. Above the noise
of traffic, of doors that open and close.

Your hoop drum in your hand, you wait for dawn to take its place
between the skyscrapers. Then as the grey begins to melt to red.
You begin to tap. Tap. For the sun. Tap. For the day. Tap.
For the beaver. Tap. For Jelly. Tap. And Rawhide. Tap. For
all the animals. Tap. And trees. Tap. Rivers and Lakes. Tap.
For Yvonne. Tap. Your few friends. Tap. The living. Tap.
The dead. Tap. For yourself. Tap. That you might go on. Tap.

Tap. Tap. Tap. Tap. Tap. Tap. Tap. Tap. Tap. Tap. Tap.

GREY OWL, 1938

Toronto. Massey Hall. 3,000 people come out and fill
the red plush seats, stiff men in black, glittering women
in fur — who squirm at the thought of snapping steel.
All the same, the applause is deafening. More.
They clap. More.

In my sweat I brace myself and remain on stage long enough
to tell them that it is time I return to my sanctuary,
for my journey is nearly over, and the beaver people
await me.

I would like to tell them that it's here in Toronto,
in Eaton's department store, where I got my first job,
and that with this lecture I have completed my circle —
as it should be — but this is out of the question.

For even if I were to tell them they wouldn't believe me.
And if they did,
would think and call me other
than I am.

CHILDREN. MY CHILDREN I NEVER SEE.

Agnes. Johnny. Dawn.

Children. Our children I've come to know,
like an arrow in my heart, as the reason.

In Peterborough with a fleeing hour to spare,
I go to the hospital to visit an Ojibway boy
whose leg has just been amputated. All I can
do for him is tell him who he is,
tell him never to give up.
Nothing more.

Children. Children of compassion and pain.

GREY OWL, 1938

Back into the night we rush to the station to catch our train
and arrive in time to hear the conductor call all aboard.
A porter helps us with our baggage to our roomette.
Finally. Prince Albert. Ajawaan. Beaver Lodge. Home.
Yvonne, I say. We made it.
Yes we did, she says, and we look at each other in disbelief.
Four days we ride — by now I'm living on a diet of raw eggs
and whiskey — on the fifth, Yvonne tells me she is ill.
She apologizes for what she considers letting me down
and says it is I who look ill, not her.
Nonsense, I say. We both just need a good long rest.
Upon our arrival in Regina, I have our baggage sent on ahead
and bring her to the hospital, where she's admitted
for severe exhaustion. I'm desperate to return to Ajawaan.
Rest, I say, and don't worry, I'll be back in a week's time
to take you home. Soon you will breath the bush, watch stars
and relax before an open fire.

From Prince Albert I get a ride within a mile of our cabin.
The walk in is tough going, tougher than I ever expected;
I haven't snowshoed in what seems like years. But
it's only a mile, I keep reminding myself. Only a mile.
And I turn my eyes away from the sun dazzling snow
towards the black spruce which become faces of old Rivermen
I once knew, and I want to wave and call out to them
that I've returned. By the time I reach the cabin I'm soaked
with sweat and on the verge of collapsing, but collapsing
with relief in the knowledge that I've made it. I'm finally
back, smiling to myself, smiling loud as can be.

The Ranger who has been taking care of the place, I let go.
What I need is solitude, to be left alone in peace
so that I may untie my thoughts, call my beaver,
play my records, chop some wood, cook some bannock,
regain my strength, hunt for meat, live again —
and learn how best to fade silently back into the bush
from where I've come. For I know I can never again leave
this wilderness. There are those who know me

as I once was and wait for me to stumble.
Little do they know I've been warned. During my walk,
the messenger spoke, and I think I understand. Beware,
he flapped through me. And I thanked him and answered,
yes, I will heed your advice, and he laughed in my heat
and whorled himself into a chill of snow. He knows
I have tried to do my best.

I am lying on the bunk when he enters. Like the wind he is.
The breath he is. Like the bird. The heartbeat.
Like the voice I heard before. He tells me to come
and fly. It's my time. Later I wake and manage
to make it to the radio phone and call Prince Albert
for help.

Travelling

When the moment comes it takes you
by the hand and you are travelling
                without a compass
on a snowy path laid out past stars
and planets, joined
                to all your relations
                by common destiny
to all who have gone before
and will come to pass

for seven generations
you leave your legacy
                a way of seeing the world
                and walking through it
you who turns to travel
for the last time
faces westward into your own life.

Grey Owl, 1938

Someone in the room at my bedside.
I manage my eyes and the room is bright.
Morning, I whisper.
And a nun in white says 8:25 and a sunny one.
A good day to go, I again move my mouth.
Your religion? she asks, and I can hardly hear her.
I want to point to the window but cannot lift my hand.
Instead I pray: the trees, the wildlife, the trail, all
that I am. Then an even brighter light.

NORTH BAY NUGGET, APRIL 13, 1938

Mrs. Angele Belaney claims Grey Owl
is not an Indian but a full-blooded whiteman,
probably of English descent,
who settled in Temagami
in the early days of the district.

LATER

The day after he dies, she is told a certain Angele Egwuna
of Temagami claims to have married an Englishman
named Archie Belaney, and an old northern Ontario guide
by the name of Bill Guppy confirms he knew Archie Belaney
when he had just stepped off the boat and still carried
an English accent. She is even told of an English wife.

His manager asks her to England to meet Grey Owl's mother
and confirm his parentage. After all she is his true wife,
the heroine of his pilgrimage, his Anahareo, she should know.
She doesn't. The man she slept with, thought she knew,
she now sees is (and was) a ghost, invisible and laughing
with great gusto. This man she will later call, with a grin
of her own, a devil in deerskins.

Ottawa Citizen, April 20, 1938

The chances are that Archie Belaney could not
have done nearly such effective work for conservation
of wildlife under his own name. It is an odd commentary,
but true enough.

London Times, April 21, 1938

Since the death of Grey Owl
a remarkable conflict of opinion
has arisen over his parentage,
particularly regarding his Indian blood.

Liverpool Daily Post, April 21, 1938

What, after all, does his ancestry matter?
The essential facts about his life are not in dispute,
for as a conservation officer under the Canadian
Government, and as lecturer and broadcaster
in Great Britain, he worked unceasingly for
the protection of wild life.

Manchester Guardian, April 21, 1938

Whatever his origins, he devoted his life
to the understanding of nature and the considerable
fortune his writing and lecturing brought him
to the relief of the suffering animals.

Winnipeg Tribune, April 23, 1938

His attainments as a writer and naturalist will survive
and when in later years our children's children
are told of the strange masquerade — if it was
a masquerade — their wonder and their appreciation
will grow.

BETWEEN BIRTH AND DEATH WAUSSAYUAH – BINDUMIWIN*

Born: Archibald Stansfeld Belaney
September 18, 1888, Hastings, England.

Down the avenue of trees, I see
a spot of sunlight.
And I am trying so hard to get there. †

Dies: Grey Owl, Wa-sha-quon-asin
April 13, 1938, Prince Albert, Saskatchewan.

*A vision whose meaning is complete. See Basil Johnston, *Ojibway Heritage*,
Toronto: McClelland & Stewart Ltd., 1976.

† Grey Owl's words recorded by Betty Somervell during her ocean voyage with
him from England to the United States, 1937. Quoted in *The Green Leaf,* ed.
Lovat Dickson, London: Lovat Dickson Ltd. Publishers, 1938.

KIM REMUS

ARMAND GARNET RUFFO'S work is strongly influenced by his Ojibway heritage. His first poetry collection, *Opening in the Sky* was published by Theytus Books in 1994. His work has appeared in such anthologies as *Looking At the Words of Our People* (Theytus Books), *Voices of the First Nations* (McGraw - Hill Ryerson), and *Native Literature in Canada* (Oxford University Press), as well as numerous literary journals, including *Dandelion, CVII*, and *absinthe.*

Born in northern Ontario, Ruffo now makes his home in Ottawa, where he is a lecturer at Carleton University and is associate director of the Centre for Aboriginal Education, Research and Culture.

CREDITS AND ACKNOWLEDGEMENTS

As a child I had a photograph hung on the wall beside my bed of
Grey Owl and my great-uncle Jimmy drumming together in
Biscotasing, northern Ontario, Grey Owl's "home town." This image,
along with the stories of Archie which have been a part of our family
for as long as I can remember, I carried with me through childhood. It
was, however, not until years later, in trying to learn more about the
history of Native Canada, that I once again found myself in the
company of this mysterious Grey Owl. Consequently, not only did I
rediscover the books he had written himself, but I also came upon
new work about him, which, ironically, led me back to old sources.
This work then is a culmination of all that I have ever heard, read, and
imagined about the man and his times.

Information on the life of Grey Owl was obtained from the
following works by Grey Owl: *The Men of the Last Frontier* (London:
Country Life, 1931); *Pilgrims of the Wild* (Toronto: Macmillan, 1934);
The Adventures of Sajo and her Beaver People (London: Lovat Dickson
& Thompson Limited, 1935); *Tales of an Empty Cabin* (London: Lovat
Dickson Limited, 1936). These works provided valuable insight into
the Grey Owl persona.

Other works on Grey Owl provided valuable social and historical
information. These included Anahareo's *Devil in Deerskins: My Life
with Grey Owl* (Toronto: New Press, 1972); Lovat Dickson's *The Green
Leaf: A Tribute to Grey Owl* (London: Lovat Dickson Ltd, 1938) and
his *Wilderness Man: The Strange Story of Grey Owl* (Toronto: Macmillan,
1973); and Donald B. Smith's *From The Land of Shadows: The Making
of Grey Owl* (Saskatoon: Western Producer Prairie Books, 1990).

The National Archives of Canada, The Archives of Ontario,
Toronto, and the CBC Archives provided access to Grey Owl's papers,
photographs, films, and interviews. While I have used some of this
material almost verbatim, notably the excerpts from the notebooks, I
have reshaped it to fit the form of the book.

I also wish to acknowledge support received from the Canada
Council, which allowed me to travel to Hastings, England, Archie
Belaney's place of birth, and meet with "The Grey Owl Society." In
this regard, I thank the society for their hospitality; both conversation

and landscape gave insight into the young Archie Belaney. To quote the writing of Lovat Dickson, I thank the Trustees of the Estate of Lovat Dickson, and the late Marguerite Dickson for her praise of poetry. The Ontario Arts Council is also acknowledged, and *The New Quarterly* for recommending this work.

Finally, I offer a warm thank you to Jane Espaniel-McKee, my grandmother, and the late Jim Espaniel, my great uncle, for their stories about Archie Belaney and our family in and around Biscotasing — the impetus for this project. I also thank Donald B. Smith for the twenty some years of research he has done on the life of Grey Owl and gratefully acknowledge those who supported him in his work. To the other generous spirits who advised and encouraged me, particularly Eugene McNamara, Alistair MacLeod, and Bernie Harder of the University of Windsor, and Geoffrey Ursell of Coteau Books, I would like to say Meegwetch to all.

Selections from *Grey Owl: The Mystery of Archie Belaney* have appeared in *The Oxford Anthology of Canadian Native Literature in English*; *Orbis, an international quarterly of poetry and prose*; *Introduction to Literature (Harcourt Brace & Company)*; and *Gatherings, The En'owkin Journal of First North American Peoples*.